The Effective CEO

How to hone your focus, prioritize your time and take control of your CEO role

BYRON MORRISON

Byron Morrison books may be purchased for educational, business, or sales promotional use. For information, please email byron@byronmorrison.com.

First published 2021.

First edition.

Designed and edited by Iulia Protesaru.

ISBN 9798726750606

Pre-order my new book and get "AMPLIFY the ultimate productivity, time and energy management course" for CEOs and business leaders for free (usually sells for $297)

I'm excited to announce my next book – "Maybe You Should Give Up – 7 Ways To Get Out Of Your Own Way And Take Control Of Your Life".

Inside Maybe You Should Give Up you'll discover 7 ways to get out of your own way, so that you take control of your life. The book is all about putting an end to self-sabotage, so that you can break through everything that is stopping you from living the life you want.

Pre-order now at Barnes and Noble or Waterstones and email a screenshot of the receipt to **byron@byronmorrison.com** and I'll send you access to AMPLIFY as a thank you.

I also have various other bonuses including copies of my other books, free access to my other courses, consulting time and private workshops for your team if you order bulk copies.

Find out more at
www.byronmorrison.com/maybeyoushouldgiveup

Contents

A note from the author

Hey it's Byron Morrison and I want to say thank you for grabbing this book.

Now, you are obviously here for a reason, and this book is a great starting point in helping you become more focused and productive.

If you're a CEO feeling overwhelmed by the challenges that come with your growth, then my Evolved program may be exactly what you need to take control and become more effective in your role.

Using my battle-tested 5-step Evolved Method, I want to help you become the CEO your business needs now and in the future.

By the end, you'll change the way you think, how you process problems and navigate challenges. You'll make better decisions, be able to trust your intuition and lead with confidence. And a result, you'll feel more in control of your life and business.

As you become the CEO you need to be to create more growth, make more impact and have more freedom to enjoy the success you worked so hard for.

The Evolved Method has been implemented by CEOs in 15 different countries. Ranging from founders to CEOs growing tech companies, 7-figure agencies, global production companies and billion-dollar unicorns in Silicon Valley.

Here's what a few of my clients had to say about the process:

Ron (CEO): *"After working with Byron and him offering the tools and rewiring my mindset, I have now come back as a more confident leader, I have learned how to defend my schedule, I've learned how to be less reactive, but to also to be able to just pause and look at situations and come up with a better plan, a better solution. I've set new standards...and I'm very confident that Byron is going to change your life for the better"*

Jordan (CEO): *"When I first started working with Byron, I really didn't feel like I was where I wanted to be. I felt like things were out of control, I didn't know how to get my life of working 80 hours and was struggling to spend enough time with my family. I was really trying to get that back, and what I found was that so much of what I didn't feel in control of, I had the ability to get in control of by changing the way I thought about things, by changing the way I approached situations, how present I was, having a true vision for my future, having action plan that really allowed me to recapture that control, to get organised, to come into meetings and be with my family, everything improved."*

Max (Tech CEO): *"Honestly, it's been one of the best decisions I've made. Certainly, compared to the financial investment the value that's come out of it has been astounding."*

Tyler (Business owner): *"I feel like I've left this universe and gone into a different one. It's been incredible...If you judge my level of happiness, clarity, sleep cycle, relationships, confidence, or every other area of my life, it's an easy win. My direction in life has completely changed"*

Rosemary (Business leader): *"I don't feel like I have control back, I feel like I have it for the first time. I used to be fighting all these fires and battles and it was exhausting. As everything felt out of my control and I was miserable. Now I feel calm and like that fire is merely a distraction that I know I can handle."*

Michael (CEO): *"I've gone from completely tired, exhausted, drained to back to my old self so to speak and with more purpose. I'm glad I did it, I certainly know that if I didn't, I'd probably still be in that state of unhappiness and stress. It was the best money I've ever spent on myself'*

Neil (Business owner): *"I now feel completely different, I feel clear-headed and able to focus on the stuff I work out that I should be focusing on, I don't jump around anywhere near as much...I'm in control"*

Josh (Business leader): *"People around me recognised that I'm more effective than I've ever been"*

Joining is by application only, so if this sounds like something you'd be interested in and if you are open to the idea of outside support beyond this book, then get in touch at **byron@byronmorrison.com**

You can also find out more and apply for a place at **https://www.byronmorrison.com/evolved-program**

Before you get started:

Before you dive into this book, there are three actions to take that will accelerate your progress and amplify your results.

Action 1: Join the Next Level Mindset Series

To help you get the most out of this book, I've developed the "Next Level Mindset" video series.

In this 4 part series, you'll discover how to develop the mindset needed to take your business to the next level.

I'll show you how to stop reacting, get out of your own head and balance short-term problems with your long-term goals and vision.

Once you implement what I share with you, you'll be able to make better decisions, trust your intuition and stay grounded in the face of adversity.

Putting you back in control, as you develop the mindset needed to take your business to the next level of impact, revenue and success.

The video series is available for free and on demand.

https://byronmorrison.com/videoseries

Action 2: Download the Resources

Included with this book are various bonuses, guides and resources to help you on this journey.

These bonuses have been specifically included to help you take what you learn and implement it at the next level.

They include "The Effective CEO Planner", as well as "How To Plan As An Effective CEO". This training will show you how to properly plan and structure your days to ensure you can maximize your time and perform at the highest level.

You'll also get access to "The Impact Driven CEOs" Facebook community where I'll be doing live Q&As, you can meet other CEOs, exchange ideas and get support on this journey.

Because of that, before going any further download and access to them at:

https://www.byronmorrison.com/book-resources

Action 3: Connect on social

Every day on social media I share videos, posts and content diving further into what it takes to become a highly effective CEO.

You can also connect with me and follow my content at:

LinkedIn:
https://www.linkedin.com/in/authorbyronmorrison/

Facebook:
https://www.facebook.com/byronmorrisonauthor/

Instagram
https://www.instagram.com/authorbyronmorrison

You can also join the "Impact Driven CEOs" Community, where you can exchange ideas, meet other CEOs and get help with challenges at:

https://www.facebook.com/groups/impactdrivenceos

Introduction

Just scroll through your newsfeed and you'll no doubt be inundated with pithy success quotes from famous CEOs, entrepreneurs and founders.

Run of the mill stuff:

"Keep pushing."

"Never give up."

"Wake up at 4 am and get more done by 9 am than most do in a day."

But after working with and speaking to 100s of CEOs and business owners behind closed doors, I know this motivational fluff doesn't tell the whole story.

Why? Well, the life of a CEO isn't that simple, especially when your days are essentially spent putting out fires, solving other people's problems and dealing with demands. It's never-ending, and there's always so much that needs to get done. Which is why at times it can feel like you're running backwards on a treadmill just trying to catch up, and that's before you even begin your tasks for the day!

That's why the tools that work for "normal" people simply aren't enough to perform at the level needed to be an effective CEO. After all, most productivity advice is basic. It's for people in cubicle jobs with linear to-do lists. Whereas as a CEO, you're dealing with ten times more stress than most employees and you have more things to get done than most people can even comprehend. Which is why picking up some rudimentary hacks isn't going to get you to the next level. And if anything, as I'll discuss shortly, advice like having a to-do list and tackling the most important tasks for the day first may actually be sabotaging your productivity and destroying your business's growth.

Not only that, but it seems like every other personal development program is all about showing up more and pushing yourself harder – which I don't know about you, but to me, it just sounds exhausting. Because do you really want to metaphorically or physically walk on any more fire?

That's why to break through to the next level as a CEO requires something different.

After all, what if you have so many things to do that you don't know what to focus on or prioritize?

What if you keep getting sucked into meetings and tasks that were a waste of your time?

What if your days keep getting away from you, causing you to have to keep cancelling that workout or date night to try and catch up?

These are some of the questions I'm going to address in this book, as I break down for you the exact process I use myself and with my private clients, so that you know exactly what it takes to show up and perform at your best every single day.

Just a few of the things you're going to discover include:

- A process you can use each week to determine what to focus on, what to delegate and what to outsource (as well as uncover what should be removed altogether)
- How to structure your days and weeks in a way that aligns short and long-term priorities, so you can sustain momentum and maximize growth, all while defending your time
- The one thing you need to do before *every* task that will hone your focus and allow you to execute at the highest level
- A scientifically proven ninety-second exercise that'll be a complete game-changer for your stress, energy and overall state of mind
- The secret to structuring a life of freedom on your terms, so that you can crush your goals, without sacrificing time for your health, relationships and the other things that matter most

By the end, you'll know exactly what you need to do to take back control of your time so that you can free yourself up from your business. And you'll leave with the tools, knowledge and mental shift needed to become a more effective CEO.

Speaking of being an effective CEO - in my experience, there are generally two types of CEOs in this world.

On the one side, you have the overwhelmed CEO. They're spending their days bouncing around from one thing to the next, feeling stretched thin, in over their head and on a roller coaster ride of ups and downs, where their role as a CEO feels out of their control. All of which keeps them trapped in a constant state of response, where reacting to the world around them is making them play defensive, when really, they need to be going on the offence.

On the other side, you have the evolved CEO. They're laser-focused and possess radical confidence, unshakeable emotional resolve and the belief within themselves that no matter the challenge, they can handle it and come out on top. Because they feel in control of their role, they show up powerfully each and every day, they don't make decisions from a place of fear, and they're able to defend their time. These qualities allow them to live a joyful life on their terms, as they're able to create the impact, income and success they desire.

Simply put - overwhelmed CEOs are putting too much down to external forces and allowing that constant state of reaction to throw them off their game. This is why even if they do know what to do, they get stuck in their own head, lose focus, or become scattered. That's why being an evolved CEO who can operate at the highest level is not just about knowing what to do. It's about having the ability to follow through, regardless of the chaos around you.

That's why this book isn't just about giving you more information. Instead, I want to ensure you actually apply what you learn going forward. To make the implementation as easy and effective as possible, I've put together a few tasks for you to do as you go through the various sections of the book. You can continue to use these as staples in your routine going forward and they'll become weekly practices that help you gain clarity on what you need to get done.

Every single one of these tasks has been included for a reason. They've been tried and tested, and they work. With that being said, I know that when it comes to reading books and doing courses, overwhelmed CEOs tend to skim through or skip ahead, telling themselves they don't have time or it's not really important or necessary. Which ironically is often the exact mentality that's causing them to feel out of control in the first place. Evolved CEOs however, do the work, as they recognize that those few minutes are where the real progress is made. After all, you don't see top athletes running onto the field with no training. Instead, they take the time and effort to practice, prepare and reflect on the past, using what they learn to ensure they can perform when it truly counts.

With that in mind - my challenge to you is this: rather than rushing through this book, take your time, allow it to sink in and do *all* the tasks. If you do, I promise you they will be a complete game-changer in everything from your productivity to your focus, how you manage your time and your ability to show up as the best version of yourself in everything you do.

Now, I know that's a pretty bold claim to make, especially when everyone and their dog these days thinks that they're an influencer or thought leader. It can make it difficult to determine who to actually listen to and trust, especially when so much of the advice is contradictory. That's why before we go any further, I want to take a moment to tell you who I am and why I wrote this book.

About the author

In case you're new to me, my name's Byron Morrison. I'm a mindset and high-performance strategist, speaker, and author of the bestselling book *Become a Better You.*

What I do is help CEOs take control of their role by evolving them into a more confident, grounded and effective decision-making leader, who can handle the pressures of running and growing a company. How? By taking their mindset, emotional control and performance to the next level.

All this started after my dad's cancer and seeing the pain and suffering he went through during his treatment (including spending 25 days in ICU, most of which was spent on life support and breathing through a tracheostomy). That experience set me out on my own journey of transformation, where after losing over 50 pounds and getting my health on track, I became a qualified nutritionist, personal trainer and behavior change coach. Eventually I took everything I learned and it became the foundation of my best-selling book '*Become a Better You*', and I started my business helping others live healthier, happier lives.

The entire driving force behind what I was doing was fuelled by my desire to make an impact and help other people. Yet instead of feeling like I was changing the world, I found myself spending my days putting out fires, solving other people's problems and dealing with never-ending demands. Truth be told, I was burnt out and exhausted, on a rollercoaster ride of ups and downs, and feeling like everything around was out of my control. Eventually, I reached a point where I was going through the motions, no longer enjoying what I was doing and got a feeling of dread whenever I looked at my calendar and saw the next battle I needed to fight. It was consuming, and a mental state I took home, as I found myself attached to my phone, disconnected from those around me and even when I was there physically, I was mentally checked out. Looking back, that mental and emotional drain was causing me to be nowhere near as effective as I needed to be as the leader in my business.

From the clients I was working with, I knew I wasn't alone either, as I saw so many other CEOs and business leaders who were in similar situations and feeling the same way. It was clear to me that something deeper had to be going on, and I was determined to figure out what it was. Because of that, I became a student of everything from psychology to mindset and high performance, all while studying some of the greatest CEOs and leaders of all time to uncover the foundations of their success.

The more I learned, the more I realized how much my dad's success contributed to him getting sick. You see, at the time he was in an incredibly stressful role where his days were all about solving problems and dealing with fires. A level of responsibility which meant he was working 14-hour days, barely sleeping and under a huge amount of pressure to perform and deliver. All of which inevitably took its toll on his health.

Eventually I managed to figure out what it really took to go from feeling stressed and overwhelmed, to calm, confident and in control. I was able to get out of my own head, reignite my passion for what I was doing and take my business and impact to the next level. From the last five-plus years of working with clients from across the UK, the US, Canada, France, Germany, Sweden, Denmark, the Netherlands and Australia - I discovered that in order for a person to reach their potential, there are three core pillars they need to master: mindset, emotional control and performance (I'll break down all three Pillars and why we need them working in alignment in section five of this book).

From that discovery and my subsequent work, I developed a proven five-step process to help CEOs and business leaders evolve within themselves to create the radical confidence, unshakeable emotional control and amplified effectiveness they need to take back control of their life and business. Which is why whether it's been through my books, coaching, consulting, or speaking, my work has been focused on using my unique method to help others handle the challenges that come with their success.

My Mission

I believe we have a duty to leave the world a better place than how we found it, which is exactly why I focus on helping impact-driven CEOs. You see, I love working with people who dare to think bigger and who want to impact the world.

The focus of this book

There you have it, a little bit about me and why I do what I do.

Which brings me back to this book. As I said, what I found is that for someone to grow to that next level, into a more engaged and joyous version of themselves, there are three key pillars to master. Their mindset, emotional control and performance. These three pillars are the foundation of my *Evolved* program, where I help CEOs evolve into a more confident, grounded and effective decision-making leader, who can handle the pressures of running and growing a business.

I debated writing a book breaking down all three pillars, but I know that a lot of books simply go unfinished, or try to cram in too much, leaving readers feeling even more confused about what to do next. That's why instead, I decided to keep this book concise and focused, so that you can consume and implement it in a couple of hours.

With that in mind, even though we will touch on all three areas, for the purposes of this book, we'll primarily be focusing on the third pillar of the *Evolved* method: performance.

In doing so I'll be sharing with you the exact process I use myself and with my private clients to set them up for success every single day. I'll also be diving into real-world examples of past and current clients throughout, so that you can see the teachings in perspective on a deeper level and how you can apply them in your own life.

Like I said – this book is primarily going to be focused on the performance part of being a more effective CEO.

However, if you want to dive more into the mindset and emotional control aspects, then you can get the second book in the series "CEO In Control". This book dives more into how to stop reacting, get out of your own head, make strategic decisions, building your intuition and take control of your role. You can grab a copy on Amazon globally.

And finally, if you have any questions or want to know more about anything covered in this book, get in touch using the email below and I'll personally respond.

byron@byronmorrison.com

Section 1

Honing your focus

Is time (or lack thereof) *actually* your problem?

If you're anything like the CEOs I work with, then I'm guessing that time is one of your biggest challenges. In fact, that's probably one of the biggest reasons why you bought this book. As when you're running a company and you have so many responsibilities, it can quickly land up feeling like there are never enough minutes and the day – which is why I completely get the appeal of anything that offers help in giving you an edge or taking back some control.

Now, reclaiming your time is a massive part of what I'm going to be helping you with in this book. But before we get to that, I'd be doing you a disservice as your coach and guide if I didn't challenge you to shift some perspectives that may be getting in your way.

This is why I want you to take a moment and consider…

What if time (or lack thereof) isn't actually the problem?

And what if instead, there's a different issue that's causing the lack of time?

Let's take a real-world example of a client who faced the same question.

When he first reached out to me, his business was going through a period of explosive growth. But with every new level of success, comes a new level of problems. On top of focusing on growth, he now also had to lead and manage a team, keep stakeholders happy and oversee the day-to-day operations. The responsibilities were a huge amount to stack on top, which was why when we first met, he was working sixty-plus-hour weeks just to try and get everything done. Yet regardless of how much time he put in, he still felt stretched thin and like he was never able to catch up.

When we broke down what was going on, we discovered that because he was pulled in so many different directions and had so many things to do, he was in the classic overwhelmed CEO cycle of bouncing from one task to the next. One minute he'd be working on a report, then he'd be responding to emails, then he'd be pulled into a meeting. He was constantly rushing around trying to get things done, to the point that he was barely stopping to think, let alone breathe. And because he was in this constant state of reaction, he'd get trapped in his own head, battling scattered racing thoughts, unsure what to focus on and in a state of analysis paralysis, overthinking key decisions. A state of mind that was amplified by their newfound growth, as the higher stakes were causing him to second guess himself at every turn, making the paralyzing effect even worse.

So, even though he knew what he should be doing, he'd land up procrastinating, doing "busy" work, watching YouTube, or mindlessly scrolling through his newsfeed. Which was why even though he felt "busy," he really wasn't getting much done. Meaning that come the end of the day, he'd regularly have to skip workouts, cancel date nights with his wife and work late into the evenings to try and catch up.

Because of all this, like so many other overwhelmed CEOs understandably, he thought he had a time problem.

When actually…

He had an effectiveness problem. As he wasn't making the best use of the time that he had.

Make sense?

That's why even though he was 'working' 60+ hour weeks, he was actually only getting about 15 hours of productive high-value work done. The rest? Was "busy" work, trying to make other people happy, or time lost where he was stuck in his own head. This is not uncommon. It's something I see all the time in the overwhelmed CEOs who come to me for help. So much of their days are filled with tasks or actions that aren't driving their business forward.

That's why before we go any further, I want you to take a moment to be brutally honest with yourself.

Thinking back over what you did over the last seven days, how many of those hours actually mattered? As in, produced high-value work that grew your business, impacted your bottom line, or furthered your mission?

How many of those hours were spent on tasks that didn't drive your business forward or on solving problems you shouldn't have had to solve?

And how much time was lost to procrastination, lack of focus or motivation?

Now with that in mind, if you're truly honest with yourself:

How effective have you actually been over the last few weeks?

I know the realization of wasted time can be a tough pill to swallow. When one of my clients had this moment of reflection, he realized for the last 18 months he'd been going through the motions and pretty much just drifting by.

The thing is though - I'm not asking you this to get you to dwell on the past. After all, what's done is done and you can't change it. However, one belief I aim to instil in all my clients is whenever you have a problem or find yourself in a situation like this one, you have two choices.

Either you can focus on what you did or didn't do, staying stuck in a mindset where you beat yourself up, focus on what went wrong and feel guilty. *Or…*

You can stop, take a deep breath, focus on the future and make a decision about what you're going to do about it going forward.

At the end of the day, the situation and the problem is the same, but your perspective and actions that come from how you CHOOSE to look at it are radically different. This shift alone is huge, as all living in the past is doing is wasting more time and energy that could be used instead to fix the problems or move forward. This is the exact reason why so many overwhelmed CEOs are stuck playing defense, when really, they need to be going on the offense. As they're stuck reacting, focusing on the past and being consumed by what is out of their control.

That's why on a foundational level, the mindset of an evolved CEO is all about focusing on controlling the controllable.

This is always one of my favorite questions to ask clients. Because whenever I find them dwelling, focusing on mistakes or spending too much time thinking about what went wrong, I always revert back to the question of: "*What are you going to do about it*?" The reason being is that thought alone is empowering, as it shifts you from a reactive to a proactive state of mind, and it starts the process of you taking back control. Not only that, but it also flips the perspective on setbacks and difficult situations. After all, challenges are part of the journey and if you want to play at the highest level, they're unavoidable. Which is why you can either choose to embrace them, or allow them to dictate the way you think, feel and react. Now don't get me wrong, I'm not saying when things go wrong to simply brush them off. Instead, it's all about taking the learnings from what happened and using that to drive you forward. When you look at problems in this light, you'll realize that even though they may feel painful in the moment, mistakes and setbacks are only a bad thing if you don't learn from them or you keep repeating them in the future. And if anything, it is in these moments that you'll have the greatest opportunities for growth, to figure out what works, or find yourself on paths you otherwise wouldn't have been on.

Like that client who I mentioned who had spent 18 months going through the motions. He realized he had reached a level of comfort where he wasn't enjoying what he was doing. Sure, things were "good", but he no longer felt challenged, which was exactly why he was just drifting by. This for him led to a breakthrough, as he realized needed to go in a new direction, to try something new and reignite that spark. A shift that never would have come if he hadn't figured out what was going on and made a decision to do something about it.

And I'm guessing from the fact that you're reading this book right now, you don't want to be living in the past. You're future-focused and determined to break through to the next level. So, the first thing we need to figure out is...

What do you need to focus on to get there?

Whenever I take my clients through these questions, they find it is truly an eye-opening experience. One client realized he was losing three days a week due to procrastinating and full-on avoiding the actions he knew he should be taking (like picking up the phone to speak to potential clients). This problem wasn't just costing him multiple six figures of revenue every single year, it was also causing him a tremendous amount of stress and overwhelm. Another client realized she was spending around seventy percent of her week trying to make other people happy. A pressure that was tapping out her bandwidth, which led to the realization that she needed to learn to delegate, let go and say no.

What I have found time and time again is that once my clients implement the changes I'm about to share with you, they take back control of five to fifteen (or more) hours per week. And they do so while feeling more grounded, more engaged and more present, consistently performing at a higher level.

Because just think, if you had an extra five hours per week, what would that free you up to focus on in your business? How much more quality time could you spend with your family? How could you prioritize your health? What could you finally do that would allow you to live and enjoy life?

Well, that's what I am going to show you how to achieve. But like I said in the introduction, this will only happen if you sit down and do the tasks in the next section.

How we are going to do it

The first thing we need to determine is what you need to focus on or prioritize in order to be more effective as a CEO. Once we've done that, I'll take you through a simple process that you can use to then delegate, outsource, or get rid of the rest. The goal is to free up the time and bandwidth to focus on the tasks that matter most. Then we'll pull it all together and look at how to plan and structure your time, and finally, we'll focus on how to execute it all at the highest level.

So grab your pen and paper, and let's dive in.

Step one: Your zone of genius

The reality is that as a CEO, you probably feel like there are always a million things that need to get done. When you combine that with all of the other daily problems and demands on your plate, it can make it difficult to know what to actually focus on. This is where so many overwhelmed CEOs set themselves up to fail, because bandwidth-wise, you're either going to be able to do a few things well, or many things mediocre or badly. That's why we need to get you honed-in and laser-focused on where you need to be showing up, what needs your attention and what's going to drive the business forward.

To do that, we need to break down what's currently going on in your life and business, so that you can get clarity on what's currently taking up your time, as well as where you need to focus your attention going forward.

This exercise shouldn't be rushed, as it'll be the foundation of your focus as a CEO. So turn off distractions, give yourself some quiet time to think and if need be, journal or write down your thoughts along the way.

Uncovering your zone of genius

I want you to imagine for the moment that you and I get on the phone, and in that conversation you tell me all about your business and what you do on a day-to-day basis.

From all that, imagine I ask you, "so, as a CEO, what's your zone of genius?". What I mean by that is, what is the area of your business where you have the greatest impact? What are the tasks that can only be done by you? Where does your time yield the greatest return?

What would you say? Take a moment to reflect, then write down everything that comes to mind.

Now, understanding and being crystal clear on your zone of genius is vital, as that's where you should be devoting more focus going forward.

To help you think about it on a deeper level, I'll give you a couple of examples of clients' realizations after being asked these exact questions.

One of my client's zone of genius is creating video content. He's the face of the brand and it is through content that they gain exposure, connect with their audience and generate sales.

Yet when we looked at what he was doing on a day-to-day basis, we uncovered that most of his time was spent on administrative tasks, meetings that he really didn't need to be present for, or other tasks like writing copy for his website.

Undeniably all of these things were important, but that's what his team was for. Meaning that not delegating or letting go was having a massively negative impact on the business, for two reasons. First, it was taking him away from his zone of genius and limiting his company's growth. And second, it was causing extended periods where his team was in limbo, as they needed his video content to be completed so that they could then take action on their own tasks.

Even though he wasn't consciously *trying* to do everything himself, these habits were causing him a huge amount of stress. By sitting down to work this out, he realized that everything outside his zone of genius needed to be delegated or outsourced. A breakthrough that took a huge weight off his shoulders and massively reduced his workload (we'll get to how to determine proper delegation and outsourcing shortly).

Another example is a client whose business was going through a period of growth in which they were doing a lot of investment rounds and his focus as CEO was bringing in funding. Which meant that his zone of genius was writing, doing presentations and pitches.

Once again, when he and I started breaking down his day-to-day routine, we found that he was attending meetings that really didn't need him in the room, performing administrative tasks, running operations and doing a whole host of other things that were taking a tremendous amount of mental bandwidth. This meant he was only devoting about an hour every day to his creative, business-growing tasks. And by the time he got to those tasks, he was mentally and emotionally drained from everything else. So he didn't even realize the impact of diluting his focus.

Now, when we get to planning your days (later on in this book), I'm going to show you how to avoid this happening to you. And how instead you can prioritize your zone of genius and the tasks that in the bigger picture will drive your business forward.

But as I said, for now I want you to consider what your zone of genius is.

What is it only you can do in your business?

And where is your time going to make the greatest impact?

The answers may immediately pop into your head, but if not, feel free to take a little bit of time to meditate, journal about it, speak to your team, or do whatever else you need to gain clarity.

Task before moving forward:

Defining your zone of genius is going to be vital for taking your effectiveness to the next level, as we'll be using that clarity to reduce your workload, delegate any tasks getting in the way and set your days up in a way that enables you to crush your goals.

Because of that, make sure you figure out your zone of genius and where your time and skills make the greatest impact in the business before you move forward.

Step two: Auditing your time

Now that you know your zone of genius, it's time to start looking at and reflecting on what you're doing on a day-to-day basis. Because when it comes to being an effective CEO, what you don't do, is just as important as what you do. This is so important that I'll say it again:

When it comes to being an effective CEO, what you don't do, is just as important as what you do.

Yet, most overwhelmed CEOs I speak to are completely unaware of this and how much it is impacting them. I'll give you a perfect example. Recently I had an application call with a CEO for my *Evolved* program, and during our conversation I asked him a question that led to a huge breakthrough that will directly impact his growth and bottom line going forward.

During our call, he was telling me about what's currently going on in his business. One of the biggest challenges he's facing is that now that his team is growing, he's getting sucked into solving lower-level problems and handholding. Now, the reason why this is causing frustration is that both the amount of money he earns personally and the business's bottom line are directly tied to the time he spends with clients. So whenever his focus is drawn to something else, he's actually losing money.

I asked him, "How much time is this taking up each day?"

He responded, "About an hour."

So I asked him, "How much is that costing you?"

He paused for a moment, then said "That's a great question. I've never thought of it like that." So he grabbed his calculator and did some math. By dividing his income by the average number of hours he works and multiplying it by fifty-two weeks, he figured out that his time is worth $1,500 an hour.

Meaning those distractions are personally costing him $1,500 a day! That's $7500 a week! And $390,000 a year!

That's a huge impact on not just how much he earns personally, but also the business's bottom line. It's not just a one-off either. If left unresolved, it will compound, and as the business and team continue to grow, these tasks will likely take up even more of his day.

If he was more defensive with his time and was able to reduce those five hours per week down to two, then he could increase his income by an extra $234,000 a year.

Before we spoke, he didn't even realize the true extent of his problem, as he hadn't properly audited his time and because of that, it was merely just a frustration he had been accepting and tolerating.

He isn't alone either, as like I said, most overwhelmed CEOs I speak to are completely unaware of issues like this. It's not their fault either, it's just a side effect of what happens when you're not intentional and defensive with your time. When you approach your days in that way, they can quickly become all about being pulled into reactionary problems, where in the blink of an eye, a week can pass and you still haven't even made a dent in what needed to get done. A prime example is a CEO I dealt with recently, where until we spoke about it, she didn't even register that over 70% of her time was being taken up by trying to solve other people's problems or keeping them happy. 70%! That meant that the bulk of her time that should have been spent on strategy, raising funds or leading the business, was instead being spent on handling issues and dealing with fires.

Can you see from that why auditing your time is so important?

As it is only once we know what's happening, that we can create a game plan to change it.

The reality is though, that time isn't just lost on other people. In my experience, the biggest disruptor is often ourselves and how we respond to the mental and emotional challenges that come with running and growing a business.

A perfect example is one of my past clients, who realized when we were auditing his time that he had a tendency to get stuck in his own head. Most of his days were spent bouncing around from one thing to the next, and that lack of a clear focus led to hours of procrastination, overthinking and avoiding what he needed to do. Lost time that stacked up to hours every single week, which was costing him multiple six figures a year!

To make matters worse, this had been going on for years. Which meant all that lost time didn't just cost him hundreds of thousands of dollars, it also massively hindered his growth and the impact that he could have been making. And because he was losing so much time during the day, he'd have to work into the evenings to try and catch up. Inevitably this caused challenges at home, as even when he was there physically, mentally he was thinking about work.

The reason why he wasn't performing at the level he could or needed to, was down to all the mental roadblocks and out of control emotions that were sabotaging his success. This goes back to what I spoke to you about at the start of this book and how in order for someone to perform at the highest level, they need to master three key areas: their mindset, emotional control and performance.

That's why knowing how to optimize planning and productivity is one thing, but executing on it a completely different story. After all, as a CEO you can have amazing ideas, develop incredible products or have a huge vision and clear 'why', but if you can't catch a break to work on the bigger picture, manage your emotions, resolve conflicts with your team or deal with the stress, then none of the other stuff really matters.

Because how many times have you started the day with a clear plan and full of the best intentions, only to suddenly be derailed by a fire or challenge that came out of nowhere and needed your immediate attention? If we're honest, probably several times a week, as that's simply part of the role of being a CEO and something we have to be able to respond and adapt to.

The problem I find with many of the overwhelmed CEOs who come to me for help, is that they're allowing these setbacks to completely throw them off their game. So when a fire happens, it throws them into a heightened state, where they then take that tension into every other task they do that day. That's why in my *Evolved* program, in order to get my clients to take and keep control of their role, I focus on getting them to master their mindset, emotional control and performance. By doing so when faced with challenges, instead of spiralling or getting stuck in their own head, they can quickly bounce back, as they have the grounded resolve to handle the challenges that come with their success.

Obviously covering all that would turn this short book into a novel, so we only really have time to scratch the surface. But I'd be doing you a disservice if I didn't at least shine a light on what's going on so you can understand the full story. I feel like this is especially important, since I speak to a lot of overwhelmed CEOs who spend hours reading books, doing courses and watching motivational videos, yet despite all the personal development, they still aren't doing the things they know they need to do. I've been there myself, so I know how frustrating it can be. Which is why I want you to know that if you're in that spot, it's not your fault, as chances are it's the mental and emotional challenges that are causing you to get in your own way.

That's why even though I know this isn't the most comfortable question to face, I believe that if we want to break through to the next level, then we need to do the deep work to uncover what's actually holding us back.

So, be honest with yourself. How much time are you losing each day to reacting to fires or solving problems you shouldn't be a part of?

And how much time are you losing to lack of focus, feeling overwhelmed, or not being in the right headspace to take the actions you need to take?

Is it an hour? Two? More?

And with that lost time, how much is it costing you each week?

Not just in income, but in time that could be spent with your family? In doing things you enjoy? In furthering your mission? In living your life?

Think of it long-term: what is it costing you over the course of a year?

And how much is it going to continue to cost you if this continues?

I know this can be a tough realization and uncomfortable reality to face, but as with most things in life, it's the challenging moments and the decisions we make going forward that define us. That's why I love these questions, as despite the discomfort, they are incredibly powerful in putting everything in perspective. Not only that, but it may very well be the shift you need to take massive action to do something about it.

What that looks like will obviously depend on your situation, but it could be anything from finally deciding you need to let go and delegate, becoming ultra-defensive with your time, or even getting outside help in dealing with the mental and emotional challenges that come with running and growing your business.

After all, looking back at the figures you came up with, what would it be worth if you put that time to better use?

How much more money could you earn? How much more impact could you create?

And how would it feel if you were less stressed, less reactive and more in control of your days?

For that client I mentioned before, by evolving into a more effective CEO, he's now earning more in a week than he used to in a month.

And he's done that all while working less hours and with less stress. Meaning he's freed up the time and headspace to reconnect with his wife, become a better parent and got into the best shape of his life, allowing him to finally enjoy life and the success he worked so hard for.

Can you see how and why it's so important that we audit your time and gain clarity on where you've been devoting your focus? And how getting this wrong can be catastrophic? Getting this right though can and will be a complete game-changer in every area of your life, but for that to happen, you need to recognize what's going on in your daily and weekly routine. Once you're clear on how your time is spent, we can hone your attention on what you actually need to take yourself to that next level.

Task before moving forward:

Make a complete list of everything you did over the last two weeks.

To make sure you don't miss anything, you may need to check your calendar, inbox, to-do list, or whatever tool you use to plan your time. It's important this list is thorough, so really think about what meetings were you a part of? What conversations did you get dragged into? What fires did you have to put out? What reports or campaigns did you work on? How long did you spend on social media or other distractions?

The goal here is to create a full overview of everything that took up your time. From there, we'll be able to audit what you did and figure out the time-killers you need to remove going forward. Take the time you need to get this done and once you have, we can move on.

Step three: Becoming defensive with your time

Now that you've got your list of everything that you've done over the last couple of weeks, it's time to audit what's been happening. To do that, go through it point by point and be brutally honest with yourself about:

Firstly, **did you actually need to do it?**

Often in life we can get into the cycle where we have tasks or activities that we just do on autopilot without really thinking about why we're doing them. For instance, they could have been part of your previous responsibilities and even though your role's grown, those things are still part of your routine as you haven't let go of them yet.

This is your opportunity to break that cycle and question if this activity was actually important? Did it have a positive ROI? Was there a better way that it could be done? Or in hindsight, was it simply a waste of time or bandwidth that you need to get rid of?

The next thing I want you to think about is, **was it something that had to be done by you?**

Be ruthlessly honest with yourself, because a big part of evolving into a more effective CEO is knowing when to delegate, when to let go and when to trust that the team you've surrounded yourself with can handle what you hired them to do.

When I went through this exercise with one of my CEO clients, we found that he was being pulled into meetings each week, when he really shouldn't have been involved in them. His COO should have been the one running several of them and others, like employee reviews, should have been done by HR.

But because he was so used to being involved in these activities, it was just part of his routine. When he stopped and took a step back though he realized that again, while they were definitely important, they were way outside of his zone of genius. Meaning they weren't something that needed to or should be done by him, which was why they needed to be removed from his duties going forward.

That's why I want you to go back over the last couple of weeks and audit your time, thinking about: did that actually need to be done by you?

Your "not-to-do list"

Now I want you to take your results and create what I call a "not-to-do list." This is going to be a list of all the tasks, activities, or meetings that you're going to commit to no longer being a part of going forward. Now, off the back of that, you'll probably need to have various conversations with members of your team about them taking ownership. More on this later.

This "not-to-do list" exercise may also uncover certain activities that simply aren't worth your (or even your team's) time and that you need to get rid of altogether. For instance, maybe there's a task you do regularly that was really important a few years ago, but now has a negative ROI on your time. This was the case for one of my clients, who initially grew his business by going to networking events. When he first started the business, this was how he met people and spread the word. In recent years though, he had not only pivoted his business, but they'd also automated the majority of their marketing. Which meant that now, for the clients they were targeting, networking was actually ineffective. But he was so used to going to these events that he didn't stop to ask himself whether he actually should! Meaning that not only were all those weekly meetings having a negative ROI (since that time could have been used on higher-value tasks), they were also mentally draining and something he dreaded waking up early for. That's why this is so important, as chances are, you'll have tasks or activities in your own life that are taking up time that could be put to better use.

Throughout this audit, remember your zone of genius and the area where you have the greatest impact in the business, as when creating your "not-to-do list", it's vital to keep that in mind at all times.

Beyond this, letting go of anything that doesn't fall into that realm or could be done by someone else is going to make strides towards defending your time. In doing so, you'll free yourself up to put your focus and energy into the things that matter most. It's important to note that this doesn't just apply to what you do in your business. Other areas of your life, like cleaning your house or chores like grocery shopping may fall into this realm as well.

Task before moving forward: Create your "not-to-do list"

Take the list of everything you did over the past two weeks and, going through it point by point, be brutally honest with yourself.

Was this item actually important?

If the answer is no, commit to no longer doing it in the future.

If the answer is yes, ask yourself: did this need to be done by you?

If yes, then, if applicable, it stays on your regular task lists. If no, then add it to your not-to-do list of all the tasks, activities, meetings, or events that you're no longer going to allow to take up any more of your time or mental bandwidth.

Step four: What to focus on going forward

Now that you're clear on your zone of genius, you've audited your time and you've figured out where you need to defend yourself, it's time to shift your focus to the future.

What follows is a simple process that I highly recommend you do every single week. Doing so will help you recognize and acknowledge what you're doing and why, as well as allow you to determine what you should focus on.

So, pick up your current to-do list and as you go through it point by point, ask yourself:

Is this task actually important?

Will completing this aid in your 90-day goals, push your bigger vision forward, or have a positive impact on your business as a whole?

If the answer's no, get rid of it.

If the answer's yes, then ask yourself:

Is this a priority right now?

Can you realistically give this the time, focus and attention it needs in the next 90 days?

If the answer is yes, then great, it stays.

If the answer is no, then it needs to be put off till a later date.

Again, I want you to be brutal here, because chances are, as a CEO, every single week you'll be presented with new ideas or opportunities that you could pursue. The reality is though, doing everything simply isn't feasible and this is exactly where so many overwhelmed CEOs become stretched thin – as they say yes too much, when really, they should have said no.

Remember what I said before: when it comes to being highly effective, what you don't do is just as important as what you do. So even if an idea is great in theory, if it isn't falling into the bigger vision or picture of what you want to achieve, then it is taking you away from what you should be doing.

I'll give you an example. One of my clients was in the final stages of bringing a product to market. After years of development and hard work, they were only weeks away from launch. Yet in one of our sessions, he went off on a tangent, talking about a new business idea he had been presented with earlier that week. The idea sounded fantastic, but there was a problem: He already had enough on his plate. Meaning that in order to ensure they had a successful launch, he had to be laser-focused and highly defensive about anything else he took on.

This is a prime example of why it's vital to be clear on your 90-day targets, as even if amazing sounding opportunities come along, the timing may be off and the better path of action may be to say no. Also, it's important to remember that great ideas and opportunities come and go all the time. Because of that, be honest with yourself:

Is this actually a great idea? Or is it a shiny object that combined with a scarcity mindset is causing you to feel like you're missing out?

If you do still feel like it's a great idea, but it doesn't build towards your current goals, or you simply don't have the time or bandwidth for it right now, you don't need to write it off. Instead, I've got a simple tool you can use to keep track of these ideas, without losing sight of your 90-day targets.

Creating an "Idea Bank"

To put together what I call an "Idea Bank," create a spreadsheet where you list all the ideas, opportunities, or potential paths you could take (you can also find a tab for this in your *Effective CEO Planner*). These could include everything from ideas for new campaigns or projects, to new ventures or hires you want to invest in. In the next column in the spreadsheet, do a brain dump of all the thoughts you have about each item. For instance, what would you need to do to make it happen? What needs to be in place first? What aspects of the idea have you come up with already? Write down everything you have about it so far.

The reason why the "Idea Bank" is so effective is that it allows you to mentally unload all your excess ideas and by getting them out of your head, you can consciously detach from them. This will allow you to free up the bandwidth to no longer think about them, without the worry that you'll forget key ideas or thoughts. Then, every quarter when you're doing your planning and goal setting, you can open this spreadsheet, go through all your ideas and figure out which to pursue next.

I'll give you an example of how I'm using this myself. Right now, I have various potential projects that excite me, from book ideas to launching a mastermind for impact-driven CEOs, a new podcast, a YouTube show and more. Yet as much as I'd love to do them all, it simply isn't feasible, especially not all at once.

So rather than getting caught up in shiny object syndrome, I took myself through the exact process I just shared with you. By doing so I was able to remove my feelings from the equation, and instead, figure out what ties into my current 90-day goals, as well as what will have the greatest impact in driving the business forward. Everything else that takes bandwidth or focus away from that can then be stored and revisited at a later date. In fact, that's why you're reading this book right now, as it's the foundation that the new YouTube show, podcast and mastermind will be built on, so it needed to be done first.

I recommend doing this task before you even start planning, as we want you to get into the habit of being as defensive with your time as possible. To take it a step further, whenever you come up with or are presented with a new idea or opportunity, you can go through the same process. Figure out whether it falls into your 90-day plan or overall vision. If not, say no. If it does (but not right now), then add it to your "Idea Bank" and come back to it later.

Again, this doesn't and shouldn't take long. And if anything, it is simply a case of asking yourself this question whenever you're presented with a new idea:

Does this tie into our 90-day targets?

If the answers no, either dismiss it, or add it to your "Idea Bank".

Doing so will go a long way to keeping you focused and ensuring you're not being distracted or pulled off course.

Task before moving forward: Determine your current focus and create your "Idea Bank"

Go through your current to-do list. Figure out what's actually important, what builds towards your goals and what needs to either be put off till a later date (that is, put in the "Idea Bank") or removed entirely. The goal here is to reduce your to-do list as much as possible so that it is far more concise and focused on your targets.

Then, create your "Idea Bank" as described above.

Step five: Determining what to delegate or outsource

In our short time together so far, you've gained a far clearer idea of what's actually important, you've removed tasks that don't matter from your to-do list and you've solidified what needs to be done in the next 90 days. All this is probably huge progress, but now we need to take it up a level.

We now know that everything remaining on your list is important and needs to get done, so going through it point by point again, ask yourself:

Does this need to be done by you?

Keep in mind your zone of genius, as we only want you to focus on the tasks or activities that are going to drive your business forward. Everything else needs to be either removed, delegated, or outsourced.

Be honest with yourself here. Is this task something that *you* actually need to do? Or can it be done by someone else?

Recently I had a conversation with one of my clients who was feeling really stressed by everything he needed to get done. I asked him what was causing all this tension and he said he still needed to book his flight and arrange a car for his business trip next week, but hadn't got round to it yet. The thought alone was taking up a huge amount of bandwidth, which was a big problem, especially since his attention needed to be on a big pitch later that week. So I asked him, is this something that you should actually be doing, or could it be handled by someone else?

That was a moment of realization for him. You see, this was one of the tasks he used to have to do when he was first building his business. Which was why even though they'd grown, it was still something he was doing without even thinking about it. Yet in the last few months he'd hired an assistant to handle tasks exactly like this, he just hadn't thought of handing it over.

By taking him through what I just shared with you, he realized that even though it was important and needed to get done, it didn't need to be done by him. Which was why he needed to delegate and let it go.

With that in mind, when going through this exercise, if the answer to the question of does this need to be done by you is no, then the next question to ask yourself is:

Who does it need to be done by?

Is it a member of your team? Do you need to hire a contractor? Is this something that needs to be outsourced?

Who's going to be the best person to take over that task and take ownership of it?

Now I know that feeling alone may be causing a churn in your stomach, especially since as CEOs, we often have the mentality that it's easier to just do it ourselves. So that resistance is normal and many of the clients I work with have an initial tug of war where they know they should let go, but part of them still fights it.

That's why I want to challenge you to look at it in a different light and think about - realistically, how much is your time worth an hour as a CEO? As in, if you did an hour of high-value work, how much revenue could you generate? How much growth could you create? And what impact could that have on the business?

For simplicity's sake, let's say your hourly rate comes out at $500 an hour. Well, then any task that you could pay someone else a lesser rate to complete needs to be either delegated or outsourced. This is another area where it's important to factor in your zone of genius, as chances are that anything outside that realm will likely fall into this category.

Let's use the client who was booking his own travel as an example. The task itself probably wouldn't take more than 45 minutes, but the stress of sorting his itinerary and figuring out all the moving parts was causing hours of overwhelm, lost focus and wasted mental energy. If his time is worth $500, then he should not be doing tasks his $20 an hour assistant could handle. In fact, it is actually a loss-making exercise, as that energy and focus could have been put towards other revenue-generating activities.

This is also the exact reason why I hired a cleaner. Sure, I could do it myself, but for the 2 hours it would take I'd make far more than the $50 it costs me by putting my focus into clients or new business generation. Not only that, but they'd no doubt do a better job than me at it anyway. This is why when auditing your time, it helps to go deeper and look at your life on the whole and where tasks are taking you away from what you should be focusing on or causing unnecessary aggravation. For one of my clients, meal preparation was a perfect example of this. He was trying to lose weight and get in shape, but really struggled finding the time to cook and prepare his meals. That in itself was causing a huge amount of stress, which was why upon that realization, he signed up to a meal prep service to sort it out for him. Sure, it meant extra expense, but in the grand scheme of things, it freed him up to focus on more important tasks, all while making it far easier to achieve his goals.

Exceptions to this rule

As with anything in life, there are exceptions to this rule.

For instance, one of my CEO clients likes spending a couple of hours a week in the lab with his technicians playing around with new concepts and ideas. Is it the best use of his time or within his zone of genius? No. But for him it excites him and keeps that fire inside that motivates him in other areas. So while ROI time-wise it may be negative, in the grand scheme of things, it's positive, as it keeps him in a good headspace.

This is also why I do all the editing of my video content. On paper, it's a loss-making exercise and should be outsourced. But I enjoy it and it's a creative outlet that's completely different from everything else I do.

Making the decision ultimately comes down to two factors. Firstly, you need to be honest with yourself about whether you should be involved or not. And secondly, you need to weigh up the cost and gains you aim to get from the action. Again, this won't necessarily be financial. Like with my video editing, the task may cost me in a financial sense, but I gain positively in creativity and headspace areas. Meaning it's a clear win.

One thing to add is that if you feel any resistance to letting go of tasks due to not wanting to spend money on them, then ask yourself: how much is doing this task yourself costing you in lost opportunity and revenue? And what could you do with that time instead?

Task before moving forward:

Go through your to-do list and ask yourself: does this need to be done by you? If the answer is no, who do you need to delegate or outsource it to?

Summary

This first section has been all about gaining clarity on what you should be focusing on and from there, determining how to be highly defensive with your time.

Like I said before, when I do this exercise with clients, we free up hours every single week and once we combine it with everything else, they take back control of an average of 5-15 hours a week! It also takes a huge pressure off, as instead of looking at this never-ending list of things to do, it'll be far more focused and concise. In fact, one of the clients I did this with recently managed to remove over 50% of what was on his to-do list!

I know at first this may seem a little overwhelming and it may also take a little bit of time. Once you start doing it regularly though, it'll only take a few minutes and could potentially save you hours in the process. Just remember, it's all about being brutally honest with yourself and what you're doing, as in turn, that will enable you to be far more focused and intentional with your time.

Putting it all together

We've covered a lot so far, so rather you having to keep going back every time, I've condensed the process into a checklist for you to follow going forward:

1) Create a list of everything that needs to get done.

2) Ask yourself, is this actually important? If no, remove it.

3) If yes, does it fall into your 90-day targets? If yes, it stays. If no, add it to your Idea Bank spreadsheet.

4) Does this need to be done by you? If yes, it stays.

5) If no, who do you need to delegate, outsource, or hand it over to?

And there you have it, a simple five-step process to help you get crystal clear on what you need to devote your focus to.

This is something I get all my clients to do every single week before they even start planning what they're going to do and I highly recommend you make it a non-negotiable habit as well. These few minutes will help you determine which tasks will have the greatest impact, which should be delegated and which you simply need to eliminate. All of which will go a long way towards you taking back control of your time and freeing you up from your business.

Share your takeaways

I'd love to know your biggest breakthroughs from this section.

What did you realize your zone of genius is? What are you going to delegate? How are you going to apply and implement what you learned? And do you have any further thoughts you'd like to add?

Head over to the community and share your thoughts, as you may get further ideas, or your insights may help another CEO on their journey.

Get involved and join the conversation in the community at:

https://www.facebook.com/groups/impactdrivenceos

Section 2

Prioritizing your time

Effective planning

You now know more about getting clear on what to focus on than the majority of overwhelmed CEOs out there and you've taken your first step towards evolving into a more effective CEO. Now it's time to take the clarity you gained in the previous section and put it into action, as we focus on how to set you up to crush every single day.

The thing with planning though, is we all know how important it is and we all know the benefits of being more organized. Yet you'd be amazed at how many overwhelmed CEOs I speak to who don't plan their weeks, let alone their days, opting instead to just go with the flow or figure it out as they go along. This approach and mentality are kind of like trying to drive across the country with no map or direction, hoping you magically find the right road along the way. Not only does it lead to a tremendous amount of wasted time, it also risks going in the wrong direction or becoming lost. This in itself adds a tremendous amount of unnecessary stress. And it also directly causes a lot of the mental and emotional challenges faced by CEOs, many of which could have been avoided.

If you've seen any of my videos about dealing with overwhelm, you've probably heard me talk about the fact that in many cases when someone is *over*whelmed, they're actually *under*-planned. This is why for so many overwhelmed CEOs, this lack of planning is the exact reason their business feels out of their control. After all, when you don't have a clear plan, your days become either just responding to what's in front of you, or even worse, doing what you feel like, with no idea as to whether it is moving you forward. Regardless, it throws you into a heightened reactive state, with no clear intention for what you need to get done.

I find these issues become even worse when things get busy, as planning tends to be the first thing to go out the window, even though that's when it's needed most. That's why I'm going to be taking you through a way of structuring your life that flips that reality around. Note how I said "life," as in order to be highly effective, you need a holistic view of what's going on around you. By doing so we'll get you performing at your best, allowing you to create amazing success, without having to sacrifice your health, relationships or happiness along the way.

One vital thing to remember is that all the planning in the world is meaningless if you don't execute and follow through. That's why after we've broken down the process, in the following chapter we'll be going through the "*Intention Reset Technique*" which will allow you to get more out of every task. And the "*Stress De-compounding Technique*", which is going to reduce stress and release tension, all while keeping your energy levels high. These shifts are going to take what we're doing to the next level, as implementing them will make the difference between being someone who is organized, and someone who consistently performs at the highest level.

If you want to take this even further, then check out my website at **www.byronmorrison.com** to find out more about my mindset and emotional control courses. Alternatively, you can also check out my *Evolved* program, where you can work directly with me to take control of your role by evolving into a more confident, grounded and effective decision-making leader, who can handle the pressures of running and growing a business.

The truth about planning for CEOs

When it comes to planning, I find the usual run-of-the-mill advice is to plan your day by creating a to-do list and tackling the most important things first. Which in theory, sounds like great advice. As you'll discover in a few minutes though, this approach can actually be catastrophic when used by a CEO, especially when it comes to long-term growth. That's why instead of relying on what works for the average person, we need to ensure that you are not only making the best use of your days, but that you are also staying aligned with the bigger picture at all times. Because of that, we'll be approaching how to structure your days in a way that's likely very different from what you've been taught before. We'll start at a macro level with a bird's-eye overview of your month, and then we'll break it down on more micro levels to weeks and days.

I'll be honest with you though. Effective planning is definitely not as easy for a CEO as it is for someone with a desk job and a linear to-do list who can map out and account for every minute of their day. Especially when at any moment you could have a big fire that comes up and requires your immediate attention. That's why the process I'm going to take you through has a degree of flexibility. Meaning that if something goes wrong or you need to change things up, you can manoeuvre it without adding extra stress or pressure. One thing we need to talk about upfront though is a common concern I get with my CEO clients, and that is…

Do you have the time to do all this?

After all, you probably have so many things to do, that it can feel like you have to jump right in as soon as your day begins. That's why I want you to think of it like this: remember back in the previous section where I got you to figure out how much time you're losing each week to lower-level problems, distractions, or unnecessary tasks? With that in mind, do you have the time *not* to plan so that you can avoid this happening?

I had a conversation with a client about this recently, who admitted that at first, he had to force himself to do this. As in many ways, it felt like a chore that he begrudgingly had to do. Yet now that he's seen how effective he is when he uses it, he feels lost when he forgets or doesn't make the time. So for him, it's now a scheduled non-negotiable action which he does at predetermined times every week.

With that in mind, whenever you feel the need to skip this or put it off, just think about how big of a difference having a plan will make. Not just in your performance, but in your headspace, stress levels and ease in which you approach your days.

I know that right now this may feel like a lot, especially since I'm throwing so much new information at you. One thing to remember though is that the purpose of this is not to add more to your plate. Instead, it's about getting you intentionally focused on what you need to get done and from there ensuring you execute it at the highest level. So sure, it might require setting aside some time to plan, but those few minutes that could be perceived as an inconvenience will potentially save you hours each week, along with freeing you up from other stressors and headaches. With that being said, if you find your planning taking too long, then that's probably a sign you're overthinking it, as this really shouldn't take more than a few minutes each day.

When to do your planning

Personally, I do the month's planning on the last Sunday of every month, my week's planning on Sunday evening and my day's planning first thing in the morning. For me that works and it's easy to repeatedly schedule, so I don't need to remind myself or risk forgetting.

While that may work for me though, it doesn't necessarily mean it's the right way to do it. Which is why instead it's about figuring out what works best for you and more importantly, what you can stick to. We'll dive deeper into that as we go along, but it's something to keep top of mind as you start to figure out how to adapt what I show you, to fit into your own routine, goals and agenda.

How to structure your planning

I don't necessarily believe in one-size-fits-all approaches, which is why I think it's important to find a process that works for you. That's why I've made sure that you'll be able to take the principles I'm about to share with you and implement them however you want. Personally though, I use a digital document I created called the *"Effective CEO Planner"*. This is also a tool I share with all of my clients and I've found it's great at structuring everything in a simple and easy-to-follow way. I also like having everything in one place and open in the background so that I can easily refer to it whenever needed. That's why I highly recommend at least giving this planner a try, as you can always experiment or change it up as you figure out what works best for you.

A copy of the planner is included as a free bonus with this book. If you haven't already, you can download the *"Effective CEO Planner"* at:

www.byronmorrison.com/book-resources

I'll warn you in advance that at first glance, this planner can look a little overwhelming. Don't worry, that feeling is normal. Once you've used it a couple of times, you'll see that it's actually simple and straightforward, especially since you'll be able to copy and paste some information to different areas and streamline a lot of the process.

To make this as easy to follow as possible, throughout the next section I'll be sharing screenshots from the planner and breaking down how to use it and get the most out of the different areas. If you're like me and you're more of a visual person who prefers to learn by video, then you can access a course version of this book at:

www.byronmorrison.com/amplify-offer

Now that we've got all the finer details out of the way, let's dive into how to effectively plan your months, weeks and days.

Planning your months

When it comes to planning, we're going to start at the top and work our way down, and that means looking first at your month. Now, I rarely meet anyone who considers the upcoming month as a factor of their planning, but what I have learned from testing this process with clients over the last few years is that it's actually a vital part of being an effective CEO. After all, when you're caught up in the week to week, it can be difficult to think of the bigger picture. It becomes even more problematic if you develop tunnel vision and allow what's directly in front of you to divert your focus from your greater mission or goal. Yet it happens constantly in people I speak to who started their business to create an impact and change the world, yet they land up losing that spark and simply going through the motions. Or even worse, resenting their work as they're worn out after spending day after day fighting in the trenches.

That's why this is a trap we need to avoid. Now there are various ways we can do it and an example in my *Evolved* program is a daily practice I get clients to use to consciously remind themselves of the bigger vision behind where they're going and why they're doing it. After all, when that greater vision and purpose is top of mind, it's far easier to sustain momentum and keep going during challenging times. There are also various other ways which we'll touch on further the final parts of planning your weeks. For now though, let's dive into how to effectively plan on a macro level.

How to plan your months

When it comes to doing the months planning, personally I do it on the last Sunday of every month as that makes it easy to schedule and stay consistent with. As for the task itself, I've found it doesn't take me more than 30 minutes and that includes the planning for the upcoming week as well.

I want to make it clear that when I talk about planning your month, I obviously don't mean having every day rigorously mapped out. That would be silly, as there are too many variables and shifts that would make doing so simply a waste of time. Instead, it's about getting you clear on what your key goals and focuses are for the month and aligning them with the events, deadlines, or activities you have coming up. By having this all in one place, it'll allow you to feel far clearer-headed and more focused about what's ahead.

When you open the "*Effective CEO Planner*" to the month overview, you'll see on the left the day and date:

1	Month		Event	Notes
2	1	Sunday		
3	2	Monday		
4	3	Tuesday		
5	4	Wednesday		
6	5	Thursday		
7	6	Friday		

The first thing to do is move the days up or down so that they correspond with the 1st lining up with the right day of the month. Then look ahead at your calendar and add any key events. These could include anything from a big board meeting to a project deadline, or life events like your partner's birthday or a vacation.

Now the reason why this is so important, is that often life can get away from us, especially when we approach it week by week. For instance, you may be so focused on fighting fires and solving problems that you forget you promised your partner you'd go to an event, or a big deadline suddenly appears that you thought you had more time for. This lack of awareness can cause us to have to work more hours, take on unnecessary stress, encounter problems that could have been avoided, or cancel the things that matter most. That's why by taking the time at the start of the month to get clear on what's ahead and revisiting it each week, you'll be able to plan around them, as well to give yourself adequate time to prepare.

Once you've done that, you'll see four further columns on the right:

To be completed
Targets
Radar
Study

To be completed

In this column, fill out all your big objectives for the month. Maybe there's a campaign you need to close out, a new hire you need to make, or a project that needs to be finished. What are the objectives for the month that need to be met to make it a success?

Targets

Targets differ from tasks you want to get completed in that they're all about the tangible results you want to achieve. For instance, maybe you want to generate a certain amount of revenue, gain a certain number of clients, or release a certain amount of videos. Anything that has a direct target can be included in here so that you track it and know whether or not you achieved it.

Radar

Radar is anything that may not necessarily have a specific deadline or end date and may not even be what you're working on right now, but it still needs to remain top of mind. Adding it to this column will keep it in your awareness, even though it may not be a priority at this moment.

Study

The fact that you're reading this book shows me you're into improving and bettering yourself, and the study column is all about you intentionally thinking about what you need to learn. Maybe there's a book you need to read, a course you want to do or skill you need to develop? Put it in here so you schedule for it in the next section.

Recap

As you can see, there's nothing too complicated here. It's just about getting into the right state of awareness by creating a bird's-eye view of what the next month has in store for you. By doing this first, you'll have a far easier time figuring out and monitoring what you do on a week-by-week basis to ensure you hit your goals and targets.

How to plan your weeks

Now that you know what your biggest objectives and targets are for the month, we need to break that down to a micro-level and figure out what you need to focus on over the next seven days.

When you open up this tab, the first thing you'll see is an overview planner for the week:

Monday	Tuesday	Wednesday	Thursday	Friday	Weekend
To do	To do	To do	To do	To do	To do
Other	Other	Other	Other	Other	Other
Targets	To be completed	Radar	Study	1) I will feel like this week is a success if...	
				2) Because of that my biggest focus this week is...	
				3) What challenges do I see coming up this week?	
				4) How will I address them?	
	Top priority				
				5) What actions do I need to take this week to show up as my best self?	
				6) What do I need to remind myself about my goals, self and journey?	
				7) Additional help and support I may need this week is...	

However, we don't want to start here. Instead, scroll to the right, where you'll see your five weekdays broken down by half-hour intervals.

Time	Monday	Tuesday	Wednesday	Thursday	Friday
06:00					
06:30					
07:00					
07:30					
08:00					
08:30					
09:00					
09:30					
10:00					
10:30					

Now, there's a reason why we start here first. You see, on top of getting them to perform at a higher level in their roles, a big part of what I help clients with is finding balance. After all, what's the point of creating amazing success if it comes at the expense of other areas of your life?

The problem with finding "balance" is that most people go about it the wrong way, hoping they'll somehow find the time or make it happen. How many times though have you said that today you'll go to the gym but then you run out of time? Or that you'd take a night off to spend with your partner, then your day gets away from you and you have to work late? Today becomes tomorrow, then the next day, then the next. This is something I used to struggle with all the time, as despite my best intentions, something always had to give, and it was usually the things that mattered most. That's exactly what happens when we approach our lives with the "hope" that we'll be able to fit them in.

Because of that, if you want to take back control of your time and free yourself up from your business, we need to flip this on its head. In order to do so, I'm going to break down step 5 of my *Evolved* Method for you, where we focus on what I call "Ideal Life Creation". This is all about figuring out what you want your ideal life to look like and from there scheduling, structuring and building everything else around it.

Ideal Life Creation

This is usually something I directly help clients with, but in order to do it yourself, take a moment and think about what are the things in life that matter most to you? In an ideal world, what would a balanced life of freedom on your terms look like? You see, rather than "hoping" we eventually make it happen, instead we need to take what we want and be highly intentional with making it a priority. How? By scheduling those ideal-life priorities first and building everything else around them.

I'll use myself as an example so you can see this in action.

Here's a sentence I never thought I'd say back when I was fifty pounds overweight and avoiding working out like the plague: exercise is a big part of my life and I like to go to the gym five days a week (three times during the week and twice on the weekend). Now, what I used to do was try to find time at the end of the day. Of course, I'd often land up working late or decide I was too tired and skip it, or I'd go but hate it as the place was too busy. I tried working out in the mornings as well, but it just wasn't something I enjoyed. What I do enjoy though is getting all my creative work done first thing in the morning, then hitting the gym as a break and coming back refocused for the rest of the day. Because of that, going at 11:30 am is the perfect time for me.

With that in mind, knowing the three days a week I want to go to the gym, I block off two hours, giving myself enough time to drive there, work out, get home and shower before getting back to work. Therefore, it looks like this:

Time	Monday	Tuesday	Wednesday	Thursday	Friday
06:00					
06:30					
07:00					
07:30					
08:00					
08:30					
09:00					
09:30					
10:00					
10:30					
11:00		Gym	Gym		Gym
11:30		Gym	Gym		Gym
12:00		Gym	Gym		Gym
12:30		Gym	Gym		Gym
13:00					
13:30					

Another example of an Ideal-Life priority is Thursday date night with my partner. I have the time blocked in from 6 pm as time off when I'm unavailable.

16:30					
17:00					
17:30					
18:00				Date night	
18:30				Date night	
19:00				Date night	
19:30				Date night	
20:00				Date night	
20:30				Date night	
21:00				Date night	
21:30				Date night	
22:00				Date night	

Scheduling a life on your terms

What we're doing here is constructing your life the way you want it to look. Prioritizing life over work is the opposite of how overwhelmed CEOs approach their schedule, and making this change will allow you to both take control of and defend your time. Your ideal-life priorities could be anything from time with your kids, to a hobby, sport, or whatever else matters to you. Just make sure you're focusing on regularly recurring events which you can build into a structured routine.

The most important thing is to make these personal times non-negotiable. Think of it like this: if you had a meeting with your biggest client, unless it was an emergency, would you even dream of cancelling it? No? Well, in this instance the biggest client is you, as without you feeling healthy, happy and in control, nothing around you will function properly. So even though putting your own needs first may feel uncomfortable, don't you have a duty and responsibility to yourself and those around you to ensure you're at your best?

Now I know that may sound easier said than done. And I also know that life is busy – but here's the reality, life is always going to be busy. And there will always be things that in the moment feel more important or like you have to put first. That's why putting it off or "hoping" you get around to it simply isn't going to work. After all, "someday" is not a day of the week. Because of that, we need to make a decision to stop putting the things that matter most into the land of "hope" or "I'll try", and instead making them non-negotiable parts of the life that we create. This in itself is a huge differentiator between overwhelmed CEOs and evolved CEOs. As while overwhelmed CEOs put things off or simply run out of time, evolved CEOs decide that nothing will stand in their way.

A big part of making this shift comes from changing your mindset and raising your own standards for how you live your life. For instance, when it comes to certain actions, most overwhelmed CEOs approach it with the mentality of it being something they "should" do. The thing is though, there's no power in "should". There's no drive. And there's certainly no necessity. Which is why it's easy to see why it gets dismissed or forgotten about. When you have something in your life that you believe you "must" do though, what happens? You find a way. That's why if this truly matters to you, then we have to change that "should", to "must". A big part of that may involve understanding the "why" behind the action you need to take. For example, let's say you keep telling yourself you "should" exercise as you feel like you "should" be healthier. Well again, that in itself is not a strong enough reason to stop what you're doing when you're busy. Whereas if you view this activity as a "must" because you need to be healthy to live longer for your kids, energized for your clients and feeling your best for your team, how different does that feel? And with that in mind, wouldn't it be far easier to follow through?

On an even deeper level, making this change comes from upgrading your own identity and in doing so, shifting your mould of the world, your beliefs about what's possible and having clarity on not just what you want, but who you need to become in order to make it a reality. That's why Upgrading your Identity is the first step in my *Evolved* method and it's a factor we'll be talking about further in the next section when we move onto taking these teachings to the next level.

For now, I want you to think of all the things in your life you feel like you "should" be doing, and if they're truly something you want, how you can commit to changing them to a "must".

I know this is going off on a tangent, but I need to point out that this doesn't just apply to personal responsibilities.

Instead, it directly ties to every area of your life and business. That could include anything from picking up the phone to speak to more potential clients so you can earn more money, to making time to connect with your team so you are all on the same page. Or even investing in that coach or program to help you get an area of your life under control. Really think about everything you've been avoiding, putting off, or saying isn't possible. By changing it from a "should" to a "must", you'll drastically turn the tide from excuses to results in your life.

The importance of accountability

This may come as a surprise to some, but even CEOs need someone to hold them to what they say they're going to do. If anything, accountability can become even more important for CEOs, especially when they have so many competing agendas and no one to help keep them in check. That's why I'm a firm believer in all of us having measures in place to ensure we follow through with what we need to do. I'm not suggesting hand-holding, just having someone who checks in and gives us a push when needed.

One of my favorite practices to put in place with clients is an agreement that if they commit to doing something, they need to message me whenever they decide not to do it. For instance, one of my clients committed to finishing work at six every day, so if he ever decided to stay later, he had to send me a text. Another wanted to go to the gym three times a week, so he had to message me if he was going to sit on the couch and watch Netflix instead. It sounds silly, but that accountability and discomfort of admitting, "I'm not going to do what I know I should do," is often what is needed for someone to push themselves to follow through.

One important thing to note with accountability is I've found it's vital to get it from someone disconnected from you. Because when it comes from our partner, family, or those closest to us, even if their intention is in the right place, our reaction can easily become defensive or lead to justifications. By having someone outside our circle hold us accountable, we can remove all the friction, making it far easier for us to take ownership and stick to our commitments.

So, think about it. Who in your life could you be accountable to for the actions you need to take? And if you don't have someone, who do you need to get?

Add in key events for the week

Once you've added your personal priorities for the week, the next step is to look back at your month overview and add in any big events. For instance, maybe it's your partner's birthday party on Wednesday evening or you have a big board meeting on Thursday. Add these in now so you consciously remind yourself about them and can plan and prepare accordingly. This will also be vital when you're scheduling the rest of your day, as knowing what big objectives or commitments are incoming will play a big factor in deciding what you need to schedule around them.

For instance, if you know that you have to leave by five to make it in time for your partner's birthday party, then allowing big meetings that could run over to be booked in right before five is just setting yourself up for disaster. Or if you have a big presentation midday, scheduling mentally draining admin tasks for that morning risks leaving yourself drained or short on bandwidth. This is how many overwhelmed CEOs allow their day to get away from them or back themselves into corners that could otherwise be avoided.

Can you see though how structuring your days in a way that allows you to perform at your best will keep you far more in control?

Prioritizing your zone of genius

Remember the previous section of this book where we discussed your zone of genius? There was a reason I wanted to get you clear on that, as now we're going to integrate that factor into your schedule.

I can't emphasize enough how important it is to get this right. It can make the difference between struggling with a business that has plateaued and is falling short of its potential, and breaking through to the level of income, impact and success you deserve.

Let me give you a real-world example to put this into perspective.

Earlier I told you about one of my clients who, when we first started working together, was following the standard productivity advice of creating a to-do list and tackling the most important tasks for the day first. Now, on paper it sounds like great advice, as why wouldn't you do the most important things first? Well, this practice can potentially be catastrophic for a CEO, since it requires an extremely narrow and short-sighted view of what's going on. By approaching his days in this way, this client was allowing his time to be taken up by meetings, administrative tasks, or other people's agendas.

Now, I'm not saying these parts of the role aren't important. The problem was that on a macro level, the client's business was going through a period of growth and because of that his key priority was fundraising and securing investment. After all, if they didn't extend their runway, there wasn't going to be a meeting to get dragged into. Yet because he was so focused on what was "important" for each day, he'd end up putting off these key, big-picture tasks; and if he was lucky, he'd get an hour at the end of the day to work on them. To make matters worse, by the time he got to them, he was mentally and emotionally drained, so his bandwidth was tapped out and he didn't have the headspace to be creative. This was a huge issue, as his zone of genius was in writing, creating pitches and presentations, all of which require energy and flow to execute at the highest level.

That's why we had to flip the traditional approach on its head and schedule the bigger-picture, zone-of-genius tasks first. For him, that meant blocking off 9 am to 12 pm every single day as time for him to focus on high-value creative work. He communicated to his team that he would not be responding to emails, checking Slack, or taking meetings during that daily period. And unless the building was on fire, he should not be disturbed either. By doing so, he was able to defend his time and prioritize the most important tasks while he was most energized, focused and on top of his game.

Now, obviously, there will always be exceptions. Let's say one morning he needs to deliver a pitch, attend a stakeholder meeting, or deal with a huge problem that came up which needed his immediate attention. These things happen, but properly planning for them or only addressing them when absolutely necessary will massively reduce the number of times your focus is diverted. Again, the goal here is consistency, not perfection, and just ensuring that these discrepancies are the exception, not the norm.

Ensuring you can perform at your best

This client determined that in order to get the most from his creative time between 9 am and 12 pm, he needed to be free from distractions and in the right headspace. That's why, to take it up a level, we put in place a non-negotiable: he wouldn't check his email until after twelve. When it comes to effectiveness, one of the worst things you can do is check emails and messages first thing in the morning. The reason being is there's never anything good there. It's just people wanting something, or demands and fires taking away your attention. Because of that, seeing these messages immediately throws you into a state of reaction before you've even started your day. A tension you then take with you into everything else you do.

This is why one of my big focuses is ensuring that my clients take back control of their morning by implementing the right practices, rituals and routines. This strategy is vital, as it will get you into the right headspace to start the day feeling powerful, focused and in control. Getting this right will ensure that not only will you be able to bring your A-game, but you'll also feel calmer and grounded when the challenges do arise.

With that in mind, when scheduling your zone of genius tasks, make sure that you consider the bigger picture of what you need to show up as your best. That may mean removing distractions, setting the right boundaries or even changing your environment. For one of my clients that meant renting a workspace with a big whiteboard once a week where he could go to strategize and map out what they were doing in a place that he was undisturbed and free to think. For another, it meant working from home several mornings a week so he could avoid being dragged into fires. Again, it will depend on you. So really think about what conditions you need in place to execute on this at your best?

Summary

Can you see how by scheduling the non-negotiables first, like time with your family or exercise, you can free yourself from your business and create a life of freedom on your terms? And how, by scheduling your high-value, zone of genius work before anything else, you can ensure you're always focused on the bigger picture and won't get sucked into day-to-day problems?

Once you've set this up, it'll become your standard way of operating going forward, impacting everything from your businesses growth, to your ability to create a life where you can have it all.

What next

From there you can then block in any recurring meetings or events, for instance, maybe on Tuesday afternoons you have a catch-up call with your CFO.

By doing all this upfront, you'll be able to take a huge amount of pressure off. You'll know the most important focuses are accounted for, and you'll also see where and when you have available time for everything else.

Why is this so important? I find that overwhelmed CEOs tend to massively overestimate how much they can get done in a day. This makes them feel like they're always playing catch-up and there's never enough time to get everything done. If you get this scheduling routine in place and you still find that you have too much to do and not enough time to fit it all in, that's a sign that you're focusing on too much or overextending yourself. In which case, revisit what we spoke about in the previous section and double down on delegating or outsourcing tasks (or getting rid of ones that don't matter).

Push and pull days

While we're on the topic of structuring your weeks, I also want to introduce you to an idea that has been a complete game-changer for me personally and that I get all my clients to integrate as well. And that's the concept of "push days" and "pull days."

A "push day" is a day where you go all out. You wake up early, work hard, maybe put in more hours, or structure your tasks around when you know you have the most energy and focus.

A "pull day" on the other hand, is when you allow yourself to recover, take some time off, recalibrate and get your head back in the game.

I find that overwhelmed CEOs tend to focus too much on push days, which over an extended period of time, simply isn't sustainable, as it leads to burnout and overall performance suffering. That's why both of these types of days are vital, and they need to be both scheduled, as well as easily implemented when needed.

When a client and I were auditing his time, we found that he was absolutely crushing Monday and Tuesday. On those days he'd spring out of bed fired up, energized and really focused for the week ahead. By Wednesday his energy would start to fade, and he was nowhere near as focused or productive. This slump would get worse into Thursday and Friday, and he just couldn't get back on top of his game. What I uncovered was that he was simply overextending himself on Monday and Tuesday, which drained him for the rest of the week. Think of yourself as a gas tank: you only have so much fuel before you need to be topped up. That's why he felt great after a weekend's rest, yet started to suffer as the week went on.

Now, a big part of the reason why clients hire me is to ensure that they're consistently showing up at their best. That's why I need to design an approach that not only maximizes performance, but is also built around longevity and behaviors that sustain energy and momentum. With that in mind, I encouraged this client to implement a "pull day" on Wednesday. This meant not setting his alarm and allowing himself to sleep in, not scheduling any high-bandwidth tasks and blocking off his calendar after 3 pm so he could go home early.

At first, he was massively resistant to the idea, and a big part of that was guilt, as he felt like he should be working and doing more. After trying it out though, he quickly found that by taking his foot off the pedal on Wednesday he was able to recover and recalibrate, making him fresh and ready to crush Thursday and Friday. The result? Instead of having two high-value days a week, he had four.

This is another example of how heightened effectiveness requires big-picture thinking and implementation. Getting it right really requires the awareness of what you need in order to consistently show up at your best. Figuring that out takes time, and also entails tracking and monitoring everything from your energy to your focus and productivity, so it definitely helps having an outside perspective. It's the same as why top-level athletes hire coaches to monitor and tweak the variables, as instead of wasting time and energy figuring it out themselves, they can just focus on what they need to do.

There is no one-size-fits-all approach to this strategy, so I'll use myself as an example on the other end of the spectrum. Now, this may not be something you expect to hear from someone who specializes in high performance, but Mondays are actually my least productive day of the week. I generally feel less high-energy and less creative, and I've found that pushing through and forcing it just throws me off for the next few days. That's why I take Monday as a pull day. I sleep in, have a slow start to my morning, focus on self-care and I don't schedule any high bandwidth creative tasks. By doing so, I'm then ready for Tuesday, where I wake up energized and feeling on top of my game. This is also why, from a zone of genius standpoint, I schedule all of my content creation first thing in the morning Tuesday, Wednesday and Thursday, as they're the times I feel most in flow. Also, if you look back at how I scheduled my week, apart from Monday, I treat the days I exercise as push days where I get up earlier to make up for the time I take off during the day to hit the gym.

When it comes to push and pull days, there are two big factors we need to consider:

1) When do you need to structure them into your week on a regular basis?

2) What signs do you need to watch for to know when to pull back?

Point 2 is all about self-awareness and listening to your own body, as well as understanding what your week looks like. For instance, let's say you're working on a massive campaign and you know from Monday to Wednesday you're going to have to work longer hours. With that in mind, you could then structure your week in a way that allows you to take a pull day on Thursday to recover.

Or, say you have a couple of days where you're feeling a bit tired. You're sluggish and not feeling your best. That again could be a signal that you need to change it up and force a pull day so you can get back on top for the rest of the week. At that moment you may feel like the last thing you should be doing is taking time off, but it's actually what you need the most. Developing that awareness and taking action on it is going to be a huge contributing factor in your ability to sustain momentum long-term. After all, there's no way you can take your business to new heights or show up at your best for your team if you're exhausted or burnt out. So cut yourself some slack, because at the end of the day, you're only human.

This is one of the key components I recommend scheduling into your weekly planning. When and where you schedule your push and pull days will very much impact how you allocate time and approach the rest of the week. Remember though, it doesn't need to be set in stone and if you feel like you need to give yourself permission to be flexible and shift the days around, you can. I find this is also where outside support can play a big role, as it can be difficult to figure out all these mechanics when you have that tunnel vision of what's going on in your own life. On top of that, it also helps to have someone monitoring your energy and keeping you accountable to take time off when it's needed.

Moving on to the rest of the week

By this point, you have a pretty good overview of your week and how your time is structured on a granular level. That means we can now shift our focus outwards to everything else.

As a starting point, based on what you planned for your month, you can now copy across and set your key focuses for the week in regards to what needs to get done, the targets you want to hit, what you need to study, and what needs to stay top of mind. For instance, let's say you have set a target of getting twenty new clients this month. That may mean you need to hit five this week to be on track.

Targets	To be completed	Radar	Study
	Top priority		

Once all this is done, we can then start populating your plan with everything else.

Now, back in the previous section we pulled apart your to-do list, delegating, outsourcing or removing anything that didn't need to be done by you. From that, you should now have a far more refined and condensed list of what you need to get done. With that in mind, you can now use that list to start populating your plan with what you need to do. In that, you can assign the tasks to different sections based on whether they are objectives, targets, or simply items on your radar (which as a reminder is anything you need to keep top of mind, but isn't a priority right now).

Once you have an overview of the week and what you want to achieve, then you can set about assigning tasks to specific days. Now, at this point I generally find that people tend to fall into two different categories.

Group 1 tends to be able to easily structure their week and for the most part, can map out a pretty clear plan of key objectives for each day and what they need to focus on. If that's you, then great, as it definitely makes life easier.

Group 2 however, is where I find most CEOs fall into, as while you may have a good idea of what you need to get done, that may change as the week goes on. Because of that, it can be far less predictable, meaning more flexibility is needed. Therefore, the aim is to assign the tasks in the best way that you can, while knowing that if things come up, you may need to shift them around.

Personally, I structure my week with a rough idea of what needs to be done on certain days. For instance, I may schedule the filming of a video on my to-do list for Wednesday, but if something else comes up, I can push the filming back a day or two. This flexibility takes a lot of the pressure off, and when something *is* a necessity, it falls into high-value work time so it's bumped to the top of the priority list.

When it comes to the days themselves, we want to ensure you're as focused as possible and not stretching yourself too thin, especially when you factor in tasks such as meetings, dealing with clients, or general responsibilities such as catching up on emails. That's why we don't want more than three main objectives in the to-do area of the planner. If you're finding yourself with more, you probably need to go back to defending your time and letting go. The "other" box is tasks you'll get to if you get time. For instance, there could be a report you need to read and approve that goes into your "other" column on Monday as it's not yet a priority, but if you don't get to it by Wednesday, it will become top of the list as it increases in urgency.

By going through this process, you'll be able to structure your week in a way that gives you a clear overview of your key objectives and what you need to get done to make them happen.

The mindset of an effective CEO

I've mentioned a few times that while planning is great, execution is what matters most. After all, the perfect plan is useless if you don't follow through. That's why to ensure that you are consistently taking the actions you need to take, we need to focus on getting you into the right state of mind. As in doing so, you'll be far more focused, grounded in the face of challenges and prepared for what lies ahead. One way we can do that is by proactively taking the time to go through the week so that you know exactly what it will involve.

To do that, there are seven questions I want you to journal about. Your answers for these don't need to be long, but taking the time to do them will have a big impact on how your week goes.

1) I will feel like this week was a success if…

What would have had to happen for you to feel like it was an incredible week? And how would you feel about it? By setting your outcome from the start, you'll be able to use that as your guiding star to become more intentional in your actions.

2) Because of that, my biggest focus is…

You know the outcome you want, so what do you need to focus on to make it happen? The reason why this is so important is figuring this out may get you to realize that what you were planning to do and what you should be focusing on are different. For instance, maybe you scheduled a load of writing or creative tasks, when actually, you're running behind on your revenue goals and need to be reaching out to prospective clients. That's why it's vital to uncover this now, so that you don't get to the end of the week and realize you didn't make any progress on the tasks that mattered most.

3) What challenges do I see coming up this week?

I've spoken to you throughout this book about how most overwhelmed CEOs approach their roles in a state of response. This is a huge problem, as it can cause setbacks to spiral, or mistakes to be made that could have been avoided. That's why instead of just blindly going into the week, it's vital you take a moment to think about what lies ahead and the challenges you may face with it. Now, this could be anything from difficult conversations to a big presentation or juggling multiple projects.

Once you know what they could be, move on to Question 4.

4) How will I address these challenges?

Again, this is future-pacing and putting yourself in problematic situations so that you can figure out how you need to handle them. Maybe you need to ensure you are prepared for tough questioning in a meeting, ask for help from a member of your team, or have a plan in place for how to deal with a particular situation. By figuring this out now, you'll be far more prepared for if and when the challenges happen.

5) What actions do I need to take this week to show up as my best self?

We all have various habits, behaviors and routines that make us feel good and allow us to show up at our best. But when things get busy, these are often the things we let slip or simply forget. By taking the time to think about them now, we can ensure we are highly intentional with them. Now, these habits, behaviors and routines are different for everyone. That's why as part of my *Evolved* program and *Unshakeable CEO* course, I help clients figure out the right morning rituals, daily practices and evening routines to keep them grounded, energized and at the top of their game.

A few ideas though could be that maybe you need to be very intentional with your morning planning and routine? Maybe you need to focus on your sleep hygiene or meditation? Maybe you need to exercise, or prioritize time with your family? Think about what you need to ensure you're mentally, physically and emotionally feeling at your best.

6) What do I need to do to remind myself about my goals, self and journey?

I spoke to you before about how a lot of the overwhelmed CEOs I speak to lose sight of their bigger purpose or end up feeling drained and resenting their business. A big part of that is being so focused on the day-to-day issues, that they become disconnected from their mission.

To avoid this happening, I get my clients to consciously go through a ritual each morning that makes them focus on what they're doing, why they're doing it and why they need to show up at their best. That intentional, conscious reminder will go a long way in keeping that spark alive and could be the difference between a focused day, and a day of stumbling through the motions. For your morning ritual, maybe you want to create a vision board? Maybe you want to read through your goals? Anything that helps light that fire and gets you focused going into the day.

7) What additional help and support might you need this week?

Recently I had an interesting call with one of my mentors. Now, this man is ranked as one of the top salespeople in the world and is a fountain of knowledge with over 50 years of experience. When he talks, you can't help but listen, as the insights gained are always invaluable. In our conversation we were talking about the challenges faced by CEOs and the key skills they need to succeed and for him, one of the biggest was transparency.

Now, transparency and support can be looked at in two different ways, and I think it's important we dissect both.

The first is that as a CEO, it's not your job to do everything, and instead, it's about bringing together the right people to create the results you want. Unfortunately, this is where so many overwhelmed CEOs become their own worst enemies, as they try to do it all, and view asking for help as a weakness. The reality though, is that asking for help is actually a strength, as trusting your team and ensuring you get the right support is one of the most important traits of a great leader. For instance, if you're working on a project and it's touching on finances, but that's not your zone of genius, then trying to wing it or figure it out by yourself is probably going to take longer, all while risking avoidable mistakes. That's why by putting aside your ego and being transparent in what you need help with, you can then ensure you have the right support. In this case, that may mean asking your CFO to attend a meeting or to take ownership of certain deliverables.

The second area of transparency is about dealing with the isolation of being a CEO. Because the reality is that running a business can be a pretty lonely life, especially when everyone's looking to you to solve their problems or putting you up on a pedestal as someone who has it all figured out. I find that this situation can lead many overwhelmed CEOs to bottle up their feelings in an effort to not let others see that their internal state doesn't match their external success. But if you look at any of the top CEOs, athletes, or leaders from around the world who have evolved to their highest level, what's one thing they all have in common? It's not how hard they work, how much money they've made, or even some super zen meditation technique. Sure, all of these can be important, but the one thing all these top leaders have in common is that they recognize the need to have outside counsel, through good times and bad. After all, regardless of how good they are at their job, they need people around them that they can turn to, who have their best interests in mind and who challenge them to think differently or approach problems in new ways. It's the same reason why top athletes hire the right coaches *before* they win the championships, as they recognize the need to have someone in their corner who can bring out their best.

That's why in my work I find that one of the most important features for clients is the weekly sessions where I create a safe and judgment-free zone for them to open up, talk about what's going on, recalibrate, vent and get ideas off their chest. This environment also provides a sounding board and prop that they can lean on, so that they don't feel like they have to get into the ring alone. Now, when it comes to support, there are a variety of options and I highly encourage you to think about what you need to keep yourself in a good place mentally and emotionally. Whether that's a therapist, counsellor, coach, or someone like myself really depends on you, just never underestimate the power of having someone to talk to.

Final thoughts

There you have it: how to structure your weeks in a way that sets you up for success. Like I said earlier, this is a process that I personally sit down and do every Sunday afternoon, however, I've spoken with plenty of people who find it a far better practice to do this on Friday afternoons, as that way they can go into the weekend switched off and ready to relax. Because of that, this is all about figuring out what works for you. So test it, experiment and see what works, as the only thing that matters is that you do it consistently.

How to plan your days

The final step in the planning process is breaking down what you do each day. In the *"Effective CEO Planner,"* you'll see separate tabs for each of the days of the week. The first step is to go to your week overview and copy across any pre-allocated tasks or activities and paste them into the correct time slots. As an example, my day could look like this, where I have my zone of genius time scheduled for content creation and other time set aside for exercise and meals:

07:30	Content creation
08:00	Content creation
08:30	Content creation
09:00	**Buffer**
09:30	
10:00	
10:30	**Buffer**
11:00	Gym
11:30	Gym
12:00	Gym
12:30	Gym
13:00	Lunch
13:30	**Buffer**
14:00	

Using buffers

When scheduling, it's important to be realistic about how much time you need, as we often underestimate how long something will take. I find that this leaves many CEOs feeling overwhelmed or rushed, as it just amplifies the pressure to get everything done. That's why I always include a buffer period at the end of every task in case it takes slightly longer. This also gives me enough time to properly transition between tasks and more importantly, to take a break.

This is vital, as I find that so often overwhelmed CEOs spend their days rushing around from one thing to the next, barely stopping to think, let alone breathe. Not only does this affect everything from their focus to their decision making; it also massively contributes to that roller coaster ride of ups and downs. Because of that, we need to break that cycle, as in order to sustain elevated levels of performance, it's essential to have regular periods to recalibrate, reset and realign your focus on what's next. In the next section I'll be taking you through a simple two-step process to use in your buffer periods that'll be a complete game-changer for everything from your focus to your stress levels and your energy. For now though, I just wanted to highlight the importance of including this in your daily structure.

Incorporating buffers will also give you a degree of flexibility. That way, if you do get pulled into a fire, you'll have some room to manoeuvre and adapt, without being completely thrown off course or feeling like you're falling behind. Inevitably, there will be days when that does happen, but in those cases, you can easily move a task or block to later in the day or week. That way it's still accounted for and it also takes the pressure off.

What's next

From there you can add in any other appointments, meetings, calls, or events. These will start to fill out your day's plan, giving you an overview of what you're doing, as well as allowing you to see where you have available blocks of time.

The next thing to do is copy across from the weekly section your main things to do that day, along with what's on your radar, what you need to study and your targets. Depending on how the week has progressed and any new tasks that have come up, you may need to add, remove, or delegate certain components in the "to be completed" section. That's a big part of the reason why doing this consistently is so important, as you may have a week where you have a task that has to get done, yet you simply don't have the time. By keeping on top of your schedule, you will be able to recognize that problem sooner and from there take the appropriate action (such as delegating).

Regardless, the objective here is twofold: to get clear on the biggest priorities of the day so that you can schedule them accordingly, and to ensure you go into the day aware of how it will flow and what is going on.

By having your radar items and targets in this area as well, it also helps keep them top of mind so that you can be sure there's nothing you're forgetting or have overlooked.

To be completed
Radar
Study
Targets

Once you're clear on your tasks, you can fill them into the available time that you have. For instance, in the sample day above, you can see that I'm free from 9:30 am to 10:30 am That hour could be used to work on projects, writing, social media, or whatever my other priorities are for that day. One thing to remember is to be mindful of what you are scheduling before or after certain activities. For instance, the last thing you want to do is plan some mind-numbing administrative work right before a pitch or presentation.

After you've outlined your day, you can then fill in the blanks with other tasks, such as catching up with emails, reading, or further developing your skills.

The reason why we approach scheduling this way is because it forces you to be intentional with what you're doing. After all, it's so easy to get sucked into tasks like responding to emails throughout the day, all of which drains you mentally and takes up a huge amount of time. Therefore, by batching them instead, you can tackle them all at once, which will make you far more productive and keep you in the zone.

When to do your daily planning

When to do your planning depends on what works best for you. Personally, with clients scheduling sessions or application calls being booked, my diary can change overnight. That's why I do this in the morning as one of my first tasks for the day. However, I've seen plenty of people who prefer doing this as their final task of the day, as doing so allows them to switch off and wake up knowing exactly what they need to do the next day. As long as you can stick to it consistently and it works for you, then it really doesn't matter. Feel free to test it and see which you prefer.

Mentally preparing yourself

If you study high performers, you'll quickly find a key component of their success is regular reflection and mental preparation, as they recognize those few minutes will massively impact their focus, productivity and their capacity to deal with challenges.

Because of that, just like I had you go through some questions to prepare yourself for the week, it's vital to do this at the start and end of every day as well. Now, I know for a lot of overwhelmed CEOs this may seem like a hassle, after all, they're busy and this is the last thing they to do. That in itself is a mental block though, as they're avoiding the exact actions that would allow them to feel more in control.

Answering these questions doesn't need to take long, but I really encourage you to take a few minutes each day after you've done your planning to go through them.

Morning questions

1) Who do I need to show up as today?

To get you performing at your highest level, we need to ensure you're showing up as the best version of yourself each day. So really take a moment to think about who do you need to show up as to conquer your goals, tasks and challenges?

2) What are today's top goals and priorities?

You've put together your plan for the day, now think about what you need to get done. This will consciously allow you to process what's going on, so you know what you're doing and what lies ahead.

3) What challenges, situations, or stress do I see myself facing?

This is so important as it will break the cycle of you going into your day in a state of response, and instead, get you to proactively think about what lies ahead. In doing so, you'll be able to prepare yourself for what's to come, along with uncovering situations that if overlooked, could spiral or lead to further problems.

4) How can I deal with these challenges as my best self?

When you're faced with a difficult situation, it's easy to react or respond in a way that you later regret or wish you handled differently. That's why we want to get you into the routine of putting together a plan before it happens, so that you know what to do. A perfect example of this is one of my clients who had big issues with communication. During difficult conversations he'd freeze or not respond how he wanted. We highlighted those situations in advance, and then went through all the possible outcomes and how the best version of himself would handle them. That removed the pressure of the unknown and he felt in control of the situation, as he was able to clearly communicate his thoughts.

5) Today will be a great success if at the end of the day I feel…

If you were to take yourself to the end of the day, what's the emotion that you want to feel? The reason why this is so important is because I find that CEOs and high achievers in general have a huge tendency to be future-focused, where they're always looking towards the next goal, the next threshold or the next milestone. Don't get me wrong, having huge goals is amazing, but if you want to live a happy and joyous life, it's vital to balance your aspirations with enjoying the journey. So think about how you want to feel at the end of the day and use that emotion to guide you in what you're doing.

6) What can I do today to bring me joy?

For the longest time, I was so focused on what I needed to do in my business that every single day just became about getting things done and ticking off boxes. And if I'm honest, this eventually got me to a point where I was so consumed by work that I was miserable and missing out on life. The sad part about this is I speak to so many other CEOs who feel the same way, as they have so much going on, that they don't stop to have fun or embrace life. That's why I added this question in, as a daily reminder to intentionally do at least one thing that brings you joy and makes you happy.

Evening reflection questions

You've probably heard countless times about how important self-reflection is. After all, it is during this time that you learn your biggest lessons, uncover what to do better and allow the most inner growth to take place. Because of that, we want to integrate it as the task you do to finish your workday.

1) What went well today?

One curse I find in high performers is that they tend to get caught up in focusing on what went wrong, beating themselves up or overthinking what they could have done better. That's why the first thing we want to think about is what went right today? What wins did you have? And what can you feel proud about?

2) What situation did I handle well?

Building on Question 1, think about the situations you handled well today. Maybe you faced a difficult conversation that in the past would have left you flustered, but you handled it calmly and controlled the situation? Recognizing that will be huge, not only for your confidence, but also for your self-worth, as it's far too easy to overlook the areas where we are improving and growing.

3) What did I realize or learn?

Looking back on everything that happened today, what has it taught you? Maybe you learned a better way of doing something, that you're a stronger leader than you gave yourself credit for, or that a member of your team revealed they had a skillset you need to take more advantage of. Or maybe a challenge came up that showed you a better way of doing something in the future.

4) What could I have done better?

One thing I always say to my clients is that a mistake or failure is only a bad thing if you don't learn from it and keep repeating it in the future. So, instead of dwelling on what went wrong, take the time to think about what you can do going forward to perform better in the future.

5) Something that would have allowed me to feel more in control today would have been…

Maybe you should have stepped away to regain your composure before making a key decision? Reached out sooner to ask a team member for support? Been more focused on your planning and structure? Figure out what you could have done and how you can follow through with that next time you're in the same position.

6) On a scale of one to ten, how was my energy?

Energy management is a key component of sustaining momentum, which is why monitoring your energy levels will be vital in knowing whether you can keep pushing, or if you need to take a step back to focus on sleep or rest before it gets worse.

7) What was my flow traffic light color?

Do you know how a traffic light uses three colours to signal and determine what action can be taken? Well, we are going to use those same signals and apply them to your state of flow, and how you felt all day. So when you look back on your day and how you flowed through your tasks, was it green, as in everything felt effortless, you were on top of your game and it was all easy? Was it yellow, as in stop and start, not amazing, but not awful? Or was it red, as in you were tired, stressed out, unfocused and didn't get much done?

Make a note of it, as you can use that to monitor your energy levels and how you're performing. In fact, when it comes to becoming a more effective CEO, energy management is so essential that I want to dive into it on a deeper level before we go on.

Energy management

We all have days when we're tired or simply don't feel as good, and that's fine. When it comes to sustained long-term high performance though, it's vital we monitor our energy to ensure that a bad day isn't a symptom of a bigger underlying problem. After all, often people can push for weeks at a time, really not feeling great but marching on. Till eventually it gets too much, and they end up exhausted and burnt out.

I once worked with a client who was the classic high performer. He believed he was unstoppable, and worked fourteen-hour days, fueled by caffeine and minimal sleep, convinced nothing bad would happen. And sure, he was fine for a while, but after a few weeks, he'd be exhausted to the point that come Friday night, he'd pass out, pretty much sleep through the weekend, and then do it all over again. Eventually, he would reach a point where he realized he needed to step back, so he'd slow down, meditate, focus on exercise and get himself back together. Once he felt back to normal, he'd dive straight back into the long hours, neglecting the behaviors that had helped him get back on his feet. The result? He created a cycle of doing it over and over again. Yet every time, the recovery took a little longer, till eventually he crashed and was wiped out.

This was a guy who'd joined a company and got promotion after promotion after promotion, yet all of a sudden, he went from being the top performer in his department, to being medically booked off sick for ten weeks due to being completely burnt out. It was at this point he reached out to me for help, as not only was he physically exhausted, but the toll of all the long hours and stress had also left him an emotional wreck.

This is an extreme example, but it perfectly illustrates the point. The problem with pushing too hard is that in the moment, squeezing in those few hours or carrying on may not seem like a big deal. And in the short term, it may not be. Yet in the bigger picture all of these issues compound, and the worse we allow them to get, the more difficult it becomes to get them back under control.

That's why I'm a firm believer in having measures in place to pick up on the red flags and cutting off problems before they spiral out of control. As it's far easier to fix a leak in a boat before it sinks than once it's already underwater.

When I check in with my private clients each day, one of the things I monitor is their flow traffic color so that I can keep track of how they're feeling energy-wise. Depending on the situation, certain combinations or patterns can trigger a pre-agreed action. For example, one of my clients used to overwork and push himself too hard, to the point he'd have weeks where he felt tired, unfocused and not performing at the level he could or needed to. As a CEO of a growing business, this was hugely detrimental to their growth, which was why we needed to cut off the problems before they got any worse. So, we agreed on some actions he'd have to take depending on the combinations that came up in his energy flow.

These included:

Two red days in a row was an immediate trigger signalling that he needed to take a day off to rest and recover, regardless of his week's plans.

A combination of three yellow or red meant triggering a pull day, where he'd take a morning off, sleep in, focus on self-care and rearrange his schedule to not be focusing on high-bandwidth tasks.

Five days of straight yellow meant taking a full weekend off, completely disconnected from work, email and electronics to detach and recover. Depending on how he felt, he'd also potentially add a couple of days on top to extend the break.

Now you can play around with this energy measurement system and put into place a structure that works for you. Just be aware that if you have a run of yellows and reds, a good starting point is to audit what you're doing in the basic foundations of looking after yourself. For example, one of my clients was recently experiencing low energy and by the afternoon, was feeling worn out. When we looked at what was going on, I saw that they were in the middle of a huge launch, and because of the extra work, he'd been neglecting his morning routine, fuelling himself with junk food, doing zero meditation and sacrificing sleep. So it was no wonder he was feeling worn out! As he had been avoiding the very things that helped him feel good in the first place. It was only when we stopped to look at the bigger picture that he realized that he'd been putting these positive habits aside. Therefore, we decided he needed to double down on self-care and by doing so, he quickly got back to a focused and energized state.

It's important to note though, that the reason why this client's situation was so easy to fix was because we had been monitoring and tracking his energy, along with the signs and symptoms that he was off course. This record-keeping allowed us to quickly fix the problem, rather than let it continue for weeks and get worse. Again, this is why it's so important to monitor, track and do your reflections, as these few added minutes can help you avoid a huge amount of problems down the line.

Final thoughts

We've covered a lot in this section, diving into everything from structuring your days to managing your energy and reflecting on your progress. I know it is a lot to take in, so you may want to read through it a couple of times to ensure you have factored everything into how you will approach your planning going forward. Also, while it may take some getting used to at first, the more you do it, the easier everything will become. So with that in mind, don't pressure yourself to get this all perfect and instead, try it, test it and adapt it along the way.

Weekly review

One of my favourite quotes is "if you don't track it, you can't measure it", and this is especially true when it comes to improving effectiveness and personal growth. After all, if you just focus on getting through the week and tackling the challenges in front of you, with no time to reflect on them, then you risk missing a tremendous amount of opportunities to learn, develop and improve in the future. Not just that, failing to take time to reflect and review also runs the risk of repeating mistakes.

Before we dive into the review process, I'll say this: I know it isn't the most glamorous of tasks. And even though you may recognise its importance, I understand the feeling after a long week when you just want to finish your day, grab a drink and put your feet up. I've been there countless times, so I fully understand the resistance to making this a priority. Despite that, the benefits of consistently following through with this are priceless, which is why I highly advise making weekly reflection a non-negotiable action.

I've found that the easiest time to work this into your schedule tends to be making this process the final thing you do on Friday. That way the workweek will still be fresh in your mind, and you can mentally digest it before going into the weekend ready to relax. The reflection itself shouldn't take more than ten to fifteen minutes and could save you a tremendous amount of time and headaches in the future.

To make it as easy to follow through with as possible, I've put together some questions that are going to help you dissect and reflect on your week. You'll also find these in the "I" under the weekly review section.

1) A few great things that happened last week were…

I find that we have a terrible subconscious habit of focusing too much on the negatives, on what went wrong, the mistakes we made and what we could have done better. I saw this happen in a recent client session. When we got on the phone, the client was really down and I could tell something was wrong. When we started diving into it, I uncovered he was beating himself up over a minor setback that came up in a project earlier that day. When we started breaking down the rest of the week though, he revealed he had had some incredible wins, from closing a new round of funding and acquiring some new clients, to confidently leading several meetings, facing two tough conversations he would have avoided in the past and a stack of other accomplishments. In fact, it was one of the best weeks he had ever had (win-wise) as a CEO. Yet, because he was so fixated on what he could have done better (which I understand completely, especially when you have high expectations for yourself), he had completely overlooked what had gone right. When I pointed this out to him he laughed and said, "you're right, it has been an amazing week," and he was able to move on from that one setback. This is exactly why we need to take more time to focus on the positives, to really take them in and intentionally celebrate the wins. That's why I want you to think about what great things happened this week. Not just in terms of business growth, but also in how you grew as a leader, an achievement you are proud of, what happened with your family or other areas of your life.

2) My main struggles last week were…

Maybe you got pulled into several fires, got distracted by several projects, or felt like you were always behind time-wise? Looking back, what were the biggest challenges you faced?

3) What can I learn from last week?

The unfortunate reality is that as frustrating your challenges can be, they are also the greatest opportunities for growth and improvement. After all, it is from challenges that the biggest lessons can be learned, processes can be refined and new solutions can be discovered. So even if you struggle with a mistake you made, remember: It's only a mistake if you don't learn from it and keep repeating it going forward. With that in mind, what did the challenges of this past week teach you? Maybe you need to defend your time better? Improve how you communicate? Lean on your team more? Or take a step back and allow yourself to become grounded before making decisions?

4) If I mentored someone else going through the same struggles, I would tell them…

Do you ever feel like you're great at giving other people guidance and advice, yet struggle to apply it yourself? If yes, then welcome to the club, as we all struggle with this. The problem is when looking at other people's problems, we're disconnected and can look at them from an objective perspective, whereas when it comes to our own problems, we can get stuck in a tunnel vision of what's happening. That's why I love this question, as it forces us to look at the bigger picture when determining how to approach it.

5) What did I learn about myself, others, or life in general?

Looking back, what are the biggest lessons you can take away from last week? And how can you use those lessons to grow or see things in a new light?

6) What was one decision I could have made differently last week?

Hindsight is a powerful thing, and it can either help us grow, or cause us to get stuck in the past. That's why, instead of focusing on what went wrong, it's important to think about what happened and how you can learn what to do better in the same situation in the future. As maybe you could have decided to plan your time better? Prepared better for a meeting? Brought a team member in for support sooner?

7) How would I rate myself on a scale of one to ten in the areas of: health, mental/emotional well-being, productivity, finances, learning/growth, relationships, happiness and energy?

It's important to remember that life is not one dimensional and therefore if we want to perform at the highest level, then we need to ensure that all the different areas are in alignment. That's why you need to be honest with yourself: on a scale of one to ten, how do you feel about these areas of your life over the last seven days?
By doing this audit, it'll help you uncover red flags or areas that maybe you haven't given the attention they need. For

instance, maybe you've been working longer hours recently and you haven't been as present in your relationships. Because of that, maybe you mark this area a three. Again, this is not about dwelling or beating yourself up, and instead making a conscious decision that going forward, you'll give this the focus and attention it needs. Also, you could notice in here trends where you've been especially stressed, your productivity is down and energy is struggling. This could be a warning sign that you need to double down on your mental and emotional health, as it's directly affecting these areas. Most people never take the time to think about this, let alone look for correlations. That's why monitoring it weekly will make it far easier for you to fix problems before they spiral out of control, especially if you compare the weeks over an extended period of time.

8) What big projects and dreams did you move forward this week?

I spoke to you before about how so many overwhelmed CEOs fall into the trap of focusing too much on the future, causing them to get caught up in the big goal of what they want to achieve. Again, there's nothing wrong with having big ambitions, but the problem with living in the future is we can overlook the amazing things we are achieving and the progress we've made. That's why we need to be intentional in pausing to take it all in.

9) Other lessons/notes…

Did anything else happen, or did you learn any other lessons that are important to think about or reflect on?

Final thoughts

There you have it, a simple weekly reflection that's going to help you fully understand what has been going on and that will enable you to learn the big lessons that will propel you towards the future. I always encourage my private clients to schedule this reflection into their Fridays and to ensure they set a reminder so that it isn't forgotten. For instance, let's say you finish at 5 pm, then maybe you want to set a reminder at 4:30 or 4:45, or have it blocked off in your calendar. Making time to do this will also help in your future planning and development, as you'll learn a lot of lessons for the future that will directly impact everything from your performance to your decision making, ability as a leader, emotional control and other important personal qualities.

That wraps up the planning part of this book. You now know everything you need to effectively set yourself up to conquer your days, weeks and months. You also now know exactly what to do to take back control of your time so that you can free yourself up from your business. I know this was very theory and instructional based so far, but now that's over we can dive into the fun stuff, as we shift our focus to what it really takes to execute on all of this at a higher level.

Share your takeaways

How are you going to apply what you learned in this section?

Head over to the community to join in the conversation at:

https://www.facebook.com/groups/impactdrivenceos

Section 3

Amplifying your effectiveness

Intention is everything

When it comes to being a highly effective CEO, intention, is everything. And it begins with how you start your day, to how you mentally prepare yourself for what needs to get done and what you do before every single task. This is what truly makes the difference between the overwhelmed CEOs who feel like their life and business is out of their control, and the evolved CEOs who are able to perform at the highest level. After all, as we discussed earlier, all the planning and productivity strategies in the world are meaningless if you don't execute and follow through. That's why focusing on performance alone is not enough, and instead, we need to shift our focus to taking your mindset and emotional control to the next level.

To do so, I'm going to share with you a couple of tools you can use before every task that'll allow you to consistently perform at your best. These tools directly tap into all three pillars of being an evolved CEO, by:
1) mentally getting you into a focused headspace
2) emotionally lowering your stress levels
3) performance-wise, getting you clear on exactly what you need to do.

Before we get to them, I just want to dive a little deeper into why intention is so important.

When one of my clients and I first met, he was the perfect example of an overwhelmed CEO who felt stretched thin by everything that needed to get done in his business. Because he had so many things to do, he'd spend his days in a never-ending rush just trying to catch up. One minute he'd be working on a report, the next he'd be responding to an email. Then he'd be taking a call, sucked into an impromptu meeting, or putting out a fire. Everything he did was a response to what was happening to him and that state of reaction was the exact reason why he felt like his role was out of his control. Not only this was chaotic and stressful, it also led to a tremendous amount of lost time.

The reason being is that every time you lose or switch focus, it mentally takes you out of the zone of what you're doing. For instance, imagine you're working on a report and all of a sudden an email pops up. Now, that may not seem like a big deal, but the problem is that consciously that distraction takes your attention away from the task at hand. Meaning that even if reading and responding to it only takes a few moments, it can then take several minutes to refocus and get back to what you were doing originally. In fact, a study out of the University of California Irvine found that it takes "an average of twenty-three minutes and fifteen seconds to get back to the task." Obviously, the amount of lost focus will depend on the extent of the distraction, but regardless, the distraction itself isn't the problem. It's the post-distraction mental state that is the real issue, as it then becomes an uphill battle to get back in the zone. Now, this problem intensifies when it recurs numerous times throughout the day. That's why for the client above, even though he felt like he was constantly "busy", he really wasn't getting much done. This mental chaos was causing him to lose hours every week, which was generating unnecessary pressure, as well as being hugely detrimental to his business's growth and income.

That's why nothing will kill your productivity or focus faster than trying to do multiple things at once. After all, multitasking is a myth. Which is why from an effectiveness standpoint, we need to get you into the habit of only doing one thing at any one time, and ensuring you are highly intentional about it.

Because when you approach your tasks with intention, you know the outcomes you want to create and the actions you need to take. And it flicks a mental switch that makes you become present in the moment, creating a state of flow that allows you to perform at your best. Not only that, but it gets you out of that reactive state where life is happening *to* you, making you far more grounded in the face of challenges and less likely to get knocked off course. Being more intentional alone has the potential to completely transform what you get out of your days. That's also the exact reason why we approached structuring your days in the way that we did, as scheduling one thing at a time will allow you to create a laser focus on what you're doing. However, maintaining intention requires that you remove anything that could potentially divert your focus. That may mean when approaching a task that you need to turn off email notifications, mute Slack or even put your phone on airplane mode. Now, I know that disconnection can feel uncomfortable at first, but chances are nothing bad will happen in that brief period you're "off the grid".

In fact, this fear was one of the biggest mental roadblocks one of my clients had to overcome. You see, whether it was from a client or member of his team, he had a belief that he needed to respond immediately to everything that came his way. That meant he was living in his inbox, constantly distracted and allowing a reactionary mindset to take up the bulk of his day. When I asked him, "Do you expect an immediate response from others?" he said, "Of course not." So I said, "Then why do you feel like they need an immediate response from you?" This exchange left him speechless, as it was only in that moment that he realized what he was doing.

The problem was he had always operated that way and because of it, he was trying to adhere to an imaginary standard he had placed on himself. An expectation that was causing him to be oblivious to how the behavior was impacting both his business and his state of mind. After all, he believed it was a positive and harmless action, that was holding him to a higher standard. When in reality, it was the exact opposite.

Changing this behaviour definitely was a challenge at first. Especially since he knew those emails were piling up. Initially, it was like a knot in his stomach, causing a huge discomfort over worrying about what he was missing. However, after a few days of sticking to just checking emails in the three daily blocks they were scheduled in, two things happened. Firstly, email took up far less of his time. And secondly, he saw that nothing bad happened if he responded an hour after an email came in, instead of thirty seconds. This in itself took a huge weight off his shoulders, with the added bonus that his stress levels were no longer being constantly spiked every time that notification popped up. This in itself had been a massive contributing factor to his overwhelm. Which is why even though from the outside this may look like a small change, for him it had a huge impact on everything from his productivity, to his focus and his overall state of mind.

This brings us to the next step, as once you commit to only focusing on one thing at a time, we then need to ensure that you are focused and executing at the highest level. This is where the first of the two techniques come in, as getting this right will be down to acting on what I call the *"Intention Reset Technique"*.

The "Intention Reset Technique"

When it comes to approaching their days, I find most overwhelmed CEOs tend to look at what they need to do and dive in, barely stopping to think about what they're doing. This in itself causes them to enter tasks in a state of reaction, where beyond a surface level idea of what they need to do, they have no clear focus or intention for what's about to happen. Evolved CEOs however, ensure that before they start a task, they know exactly what they need to get done and how they're going to do it. They recognize that in doing so, not only will they execute at a higher level, they'll also make better use of their time, make better decisions and feel more prepared for challenges that could come up.

That's why before you begin any new task - whether it's a meeting, responding to emails, working on a report or whatever else you need to get done, we need to get you clear on what you're about to do.

To start, take 30 to 90 seconds where you stop and visualize what you're about to get done. Mentally take yourself through the action from start to finish, thinking about what you need to do. What is the outcome you want to create? How do you need to approach the task to ensure you're executing it as your best self? What possible challenges, fires or obstacles may come up? And how will you deal with them if they do?

Now I know what you're thinking, "Byron, there's no way I have time to spend 90 seconds before every task doing this visualization stuff". Well, that's exactly what one of my clients thought back when she was an overwhelmed CEO. After trying it though, she found that those few minutes to set her intention meant she went into tasks more focused and engaged. And because of it, she lost less time to procrastination and overthinking, all while feeling less overwhelmed and more in control of her days. Now, this is so important, that instead of just glossing over it, I want us to instead look at it on a deeper level.

The power of visualization

From the outside, visualization may sound like some woo woo spiritual practice, and I'll be the first to admit that when I first learned about this, I thought it was silly. The reality is though that we often dismiss what we don't understand, and actually, visualization is a scientifically proven concept and an incredibly powerful tool.

To put it simply, your brain has a network of neurons in what is called your Reticular Activating System. Essentially, this is a filter system that allows certain information into your brain, all while blocking out other information. The filter itself is influenced by your subconscious, which has been programmed since a young age from the environments, people, events, circumstances and situations you went through. All of these shape your mould of the world, creating a lens if you will, of the reality you believe is true. It's important to note that this mould of the world is different for everyone, after all, we've all led different lives and because of it, we view the world through different lenses.

And this is so important to understand, as our beliefs can either cause suffering or benefit. At the root cause level, your beliefs dictate everything from your decision making to your self-worth, how you connect with others, when you put yourself out there, how you respond to criticism or how you persevere in challenging times. And because they are unconscious thought patterns, unless we watch out for them or catch ourselves in the act, we can be completely oblivious to what's going on and how they're influencing the way we think, feel or behave. For instance, do you know how at the first sign of resistance some people quit and give up, immediately going into all sorts of excuses about how it can't be done? That may well be down to their subconscious programming convincing them it simply isn't possible, or that because they failed once, they're destined to fail again.

One of my favourite stories that puts this into perspective is the story of the elephant and the peg. There's a baby elephant in a zoo and at a young age, the zookeepers tied it to a peg in the ground that's strong enough that it stops it from moving away. Even when the elephant gets older and stronger, and could easily rip that peg out of the ground, the zookeepers never have to change the weight of it. Why? Because the elephant made a decision and took on a belief when it was younger that it couldn't break free, so it doesn't even try. All because it has a story in its head about its own limitations, what it can and can't do and the reality in which it lives.

The reason why we all have this chunked down mould of the world is that there are millions of things going on around you at any one time, from the taste in your mouth, to the feel of your shirt on your body, to smells and sounds. If your brain tried to process all of them at once, it would explode, which is why instead, your Reticular Activating System filters, chunks and breaks down what's going on around you based on what's important to you.

This is why if you ever thought of buying a new car, suddenly you see it wherever you go. Or you buy a new shirt, and everyone else seems to be wearing it. It's not that it wasn't there before, it just wasn't important to you. So your brain filtered it out and instead bases your focus on information that supports your mould of the world. And this is vital to know if you want to be able to consciously address any biases or limiting beliefs that might be holding you back.

Because let's say you struggle with confidence. Throughout the day, your Reticular Activating System will be searching and bringing into awareness anything that happens which supports the belief that you have. As I mentioned before, this can either be positive or negative, as it'll either cause you to be focusing on situations, behaviours or thoughts that drive you forward, or sabotaging thoughts that hold you back.

Now, this is something that happens to all of us in different areas of our lives, which is why it's so important to realize – you are not your beliefs, they're just stories in your head that have been created in your subconscious from what has happened to you in your life. And this is where so many people get trapped, as they're so focused on the past and what happened, that like the elephant with the peg, they allow that story in their head to directly impact how they think, feel and behave today.

The thing is though, you can't change the past, but what you can do is change how you respond to it. That's why if you can change your story, you can change your life, as you can start to see and believe that your past doesn't have to define your future. That realization in itself is incredibly empowering and I've found for a lot of people it's the exact shift they need within themselves to move forward and into the next level of their lives.

A big part of that process is using visualization to reprogram your Reticular Activating System, so that your brain shifts its focus to looking for evidence and events that support the new beliefs you want to take on. For instance, when one of my clients first started working with me, he had a belief that he wasn't good at doing pitches or presentations. And because of that belief, before going into a meeting or talk, his subconscious programming would cause him to focus on how he was going to fail and mess up. So, what do you think happened? Well, because he was fixated on how it was going to go wrong, that it caused all this anxious energy to build up inside him. So he'd mumble his words and lose his train of thought – landing up in a self-sabotaging and self-fulfilling prophecy, where his actions and behaviours would align with the beliefs in his head, creating the outcome he had initially feared. In turn, this just supported those beliefs, reaffirming that he wasn't good at presentations.

That's why when it came to the next pitch, we flipped it. I got him to visualize and play out the event in his mind, where instead of focusing on how he was going to fail, he visualized himself showing up powerfully, walking in full of confidence and keeping calm and composed in the face of questioning. He imagined that his presenting was engaging, full of passion and excitement. The result? He was able to walk into the room and follow through with what he imagined, dominating that presentation and closing a huge new round of funding. The best part though was that after he did it once, it then gave his brain new supporting evidence that actually, he was great at presentations. Meaning he became more confident in his own ability and every time he was in the same situation it became easier to repeat the process, until those beliefs eventually became his new default programming.

How to do this based on science

Now, to effectively use visualization, there are two science-backed steps you need to go through.

Let's say your goal is to become a more confident CEO. Firstly, you need to visualize what your life would look like if that happened and how you're going to feel about yourself when you have that new level of confidence.

To visualize you need to close your eyes, and from there get a clear and specific picture of what it looks like when your confidence has improved. See yourself confidently making decisions, speaking up from your own intuition in that meeting, facing that difficult conversation instead of avoiding it, walking into that presentation and dominating it. Whatever that may look like for you, you need to see yourself doing it.

Once you start to visualize that image, step two is to consciously think about the emotions you're going to feel.

Now, it's vital here that the emotions you think of are positive, whether that's feeling in control, grounded, happy, joyous or whatever it may be. You need to match these emotions to the image in your head, because when you do, you'll start to train your brain to change its filter. The reason being is it's been proven our brains can't tell the difference between the reality of what actually happened and what we imagine. Meaning it can't tell the difference between the memories you have of the past and the imagined visualizations you're creating. Therefore visualizing the actions you want to take will allow you to take it on as a new memory. This in turn will then start to change your mould of the world and the beliefs you have about what you can and can't do. Now, it's important to remember that your beliefs have formed over the years and are deeply ingrained within you. Because of that, even though this practice may spike a feel-good dopamine hit, doing this just once is not enough to create long-lasting change. Instead, it needs to be repeated regularly if you truly want to change the story in your head. Research has even shown that the more you use this practice and visualize what you want, the more it becomes your reality.

With that in mind, even though the goal of visualization is to create clarity, it's important to note, that clarity alone doesn't lead to growth or transformation. And instead, it is what you do with that clarity that really makes the difference. Therefore, in order to create the greatest impact, you need to become congruent with the vision you create, aligning it with the best version of yourself - and most importantly, living as that version consistently.

This is the reason why one of the first things I do with all new clients is to help them figure out who they need to become to create the life, results and success they desire. Getting them clear on who that next level version of themselves is, who every single day shows up powerfully, has unstoppable confidence in themselves, who can lead and influence those around them and is able to create a life of freedom on their terms. By getting them clear on who they need to become, we can do two things. First, we can reverse engineer the journey, creating a step-by-step plan where they take on the habits, behaviours and the non-negotiable parts of their day that they need to step into to close the gap. And secondly, we can then use that clarity to create a morning visualization practice where they can consciously take themselves through imagining that they are already that person, that they've already achieved those goals, and that life is actually a reality. Now getting this right is a process I need to take you through, which is why it is out of the scope of this book. However, if it is something you want to incorporate into your own life, I do cover that exact process in both my *Evolved* program, as well as my *Unshakeable* CEO course.

You can find out more about the *Unshakeable* CEO course at:

www.byronmorrison.com/unshakeable-ceo-offer

Or the Evolved coaching program at:

https://www.byronmorrison.com/evolved-program

What this means for your effectiveness

What I've gone through goes back to what I said to you at the start of this section – intention is everything. And it begins with starting your day by visualizing what you need to get done, how you're going to crush your goals and how you're going to feel when it's all done. From there, it then continues with how you go into every task and how to transition between actions throughout the day.

Not only is this going to allow you to mentally feel more prepared, but studies have also shown that creating that visualized image in your mind, actually allows you to develop and improve the skills, just like if you were actually doing it. That's why doing this on a regular basis will allow you to change that network of neurons in your Reticular Activating System, thereby reprogramming your subconscious and the filter through which you view the world.

Now like I said before, this doesn't need to take long. Before every task, take 30 to 90 seconds to take yourself through what you need to get done. What's the outcome you want to create? Who do you need to show up as? What challenges will you need to overcome? How do you need to handle them as your best self? And how will it feel when you achieve what you set out to do?

The purpose of this is to get you out of that reactive state of response, where instead of going in blind, you're proactively prepared for exactly what you need to do. By taking the time to stop and think about what you're doing, you'll also potentially avoid all sorts of headaches or mistakes that could have happened if you just dived straight in.

This applies to everything from working on that report, to conversations with your team, pitches, meetings and every other part of your day. For instance, how many times have you gone into a meeting to discuss hitting a particular target, and all of a sudden everyone's debating the colour of the font on the letterhead? Or started working on a report only to lose your train of thought and completely forget what you were trying to get out of it?

We've all been there, and I regularly speak to overwhelmed CEOs who are allowing these unfocused tasks to consume hours of their time and bandwidth every week. That's why by setting your intention up front, you can know exactly what you want to accomplish. In the case of a meeting, doing so can allow you to set a clear agenda, where everyone knows the purpose of it and it can immediately be pulled back on track whenever it goes off course. Meaning those 90 seconds you took to mentally prepare yourself, could turn that meeting which would previously have taken an hour into 15 minutes of highly focused time.

Let's say you need to have a difficult conversation with a member of your team. For one of my clients, this was the part of the role she'd dread the most. So much so, that she'd avoid challenging conversations for weeks, if not months at a time. The reason being was that these meetings had a tendency to spiral and bring in lots of highly charged emotions, making these meetings extremely frustrating and draining. The problem with going into conversations in a state of response, is it's far too easy for them to escalate. Whereas instead, I got her to mentally take herself through the conversation in advance. How did she need to approach it? What did she need to say? What were the possible responses the other person could make? And how would the evolved, best version of herself respond to them? Not only did this ease a tremendous amount of tension, it also meant that she knew how to deal with reactive situations, as she had prepared herself ahead of time.

This also works amazingly in situations where you need to bring your A-game. For instance, I mentioned that client who got nervous before pitches. In the past, those few minutes before would cause all this anxious energy to build up inside him, which in turn would throw him off his game. That's why we created a ritual where 5 minutes before a pitch or presentation, he'd close his eyes, go through the breathing exercise I'll share with you in the next section and then visualize the first few minutes of the talk. Going through how he needed to start, who he needed to show up as, the pace he spoke, how he stood and what he needed to say. This took him from nervous to unshakeable confidence, as he was then able to walk into that room full of intention and mentally in a zone where he could then execute on autopilot.

This is the exact same reason why elite athletes mentally take themselves through that shot before they take it. As by visualizing what they want and the outcome they want to create, it makes it far more likely they'll be able to follow through when it matters most.

Make sense?

Setting intention in other areas of your life

Setting your intention doesn't just apply to how you approach work-related tasks and instead, it's an invaluable practice to use in other areas of your life as well. After all, how many times have you got home from a long day, with so much on your mind that you're consumed by the thought of work? So even though you're physically sitting there with your partner talking about their day, you're zoned out, not present or really listening? This was something I used to struggle with all the time, and that lack of intention is why so many overwhelmed CEOs land up feeling disconnected from those around them or having problems in their relationships.

In running a big tech company, one of my clients was facing so many competing agendas and demands, that he found himself constantly rushing around throughout the day. Mentally, he was always wired, trying to process a 1000 racing thoughts that at times would cause heightened emotions and overwhelm. A feeling he'd then carry with him into his commute, where sitting in traffic would cause him to feel even more frustrated and on edge. He'd get home, walk through the door and still feel stressed thinking about his day. Because of his workload, it also meant he regularly needed to work evenings to try and catch up. Which in turn caused him to be mentally preoccupied about what he still needed to get done before he could finish his day. This meant that he'd sit at the dinner table attached to his phone, barely saying a word and consumed by what was going on in his head. And it was so frustrating for him, as he wanted nothing more than to be present and in the moment with his family. Yet he just couldn't shake the racing thoughts in his head. You see, the problem was he was carrying the baggage of his day with him, as he hadn't taken a moment to de-load.

We had to introduce a strategy in his routine to help him leave work at work and be present at home. That's why when he pulled into the driveway feeling stressed from his commute, instead of rushing into the house and taking that tension with him, he needed to take a moment to ground himself and let it go. That's why we created a ritual where he'd spend a few minutes still in the car to stop and go through the "Stress De-compounding Technique" I'll be sharing with you in the next section. He'd then visualize and set his intention for what he was about to do; thinking about how he wanted to walk through the front door. Was it as that stressed and overwhelmed CEO? Or as that happy to see his family, engaged husband and parent? How did he want to use the next hour of his time? How did he want to behave in the moment?

Cause here's the thing, an hour of focused intention of being in the moment is far more valuable than 4 hours of being mentally checked out. So even on nights he had to continue working, he could come home, have an hour's quality time with the family, and then go finish up on a few things in his office. A shift that reignited his marriage, reconnected him with his kids and released him from a whole weight of guilt. All from taking a few short minutes to stop, breath and get clear on what he needed to do.

Now you may be thinking, what does this have to do with being a more effective CEO? And the answer is – everything. Because at the end of the day, if you have issues in other areas of your life, they can and will directly impact your performance as a CEO.

Overwhelmed CEOs allow themselves to be at the mercy of the moment, letting how they feel and their thoughts control how they behave. Whereas Evolved CEOs recognize that having that deeper level of connection, engagement and purpose, directly comes from being intentional in everything they do. As when you start living a life full of intention, you can start to feel more of your day. You can start to embrace more of what's going on around you. You can start to be more present in moments, have more joy, feel closer to those around you and feel more in control. And ultimately, this is how you live a more fulfilled and happy life.

That's why regardless of what you're doing, it's so important to set your intention for who you want to be in that moment. Thinking about everything from who you need to show up as, to who you need to give your attention to. How do you need to be present, how can you engage with those around you and who is that higher level, more vibrant version of yourself?

Here's a challenge for you.

Commit to taking 30 to 90 seconds before all big tasks, events or activities to think about what's your intention? What's the outcome that you want to create? What possible challenges could get in the way? And how are you going to face them as the best version of you? Do this regularly and you'll see a complete change in how you approach and live your life.

Releasing tension

The reality is that running a business is a rollercoaster of ups and downs, where one moment you can feel on top of the world, and the next like everything is falling apart. It truly is a never-ending ride and one which unfortunately for better or worse, is simply part of the role of being a CEO. The problem for so many overwhelmed CEOs though is this daily cycle causes them to spiral out of control. And as a result, it keeps them trapped in a state of response, where it's only a matter of time before reacting to the world around them causes their emotions to take over and get the better of them (usually in the form of frustration, anger, overwhelm, anxiety or some other negative emotional state).

There's a reason why this is happening and one of my old clients is a perfect example of it. I still remember the first phone call she and I had. We'd been chatting on email and messages for months, and she wanted to work with me, but she kept putting it off as she felt like she had too much on and it wasn't the right time. One morning though I got a scheduling email come through that she'd booked a call to speak to me. Now, I knew from our previous messages that time had been a barrier in the past, so when we got on the call, I was curious, so I asked her, "why now?"

She started telling me about how the day before she went to the pharmacy to pick up a prescription. Yet when she got there, she found out she had the wrong day and it wouldn't be available until tomorrow. Now, apart from the minor inconvenience, in the grand scheme of things, this really wasn't a big deal. But she got back in her car and out of nowhere completely broke down in tears. This wasn't the first time either, as recently the smallest things seemed to be getting to her. Which was why she reached out to me, as she just couldn't understand why this was happening.

From the outside, it was obvious something deeper was going on, so we started talking more about her life and what she did on a daily basis. What I found was that like most CEOs, her days were essentially putting out fires, solving other people's problems and dealing with never-ending demands. An ordeal that started from the moment she woke up, as she'd immediately open her phone and face a barrage of emails and fires that built up overnight. It then continued when she got to work, as everyone was constantly turning to her to solve their problems. It was non-stop, to the point that she was pretty much just bouncing from one challenge to the next.

Now, the problem with this is that when you're facing all of these stressors throughout the day, that tension compounds and builds up inside you, till eventually it gets too much and you can't hold it in anymore. This was the exact reason why the pharmacy incident set her off. In isolation it wasn't a big deal, but when stacked on top of everything else that happened it was the tipping point that pushed her over the edge.

And she's not alone, as I see this all the time in the clients I work with. From people losing their temper with their team, to firing from the hip when confronted in a difficult situation, or getting upset when something goes wrong. All of those emotions build up inside them, till eventually, they react in a way that feels out of their control.

Think of it like a gas tank, where every fire, challenging email, difficult conversation, setback or stressor from what you need to get done starts to fill it, compounding and stacking on top of what was already in there. Till eventually, there's simply no more room in the tank and it explodes.

Well, in order to avoid this, we need to regularly and intentionally release the tension at routine intervals throughout the day. Now, with my clients, there are various tools and practices we use to make this happen, one of which I call the *"Stress De-compounding Technique"*.

The Stress De-compounding Technique

This is a scientifically proven practice to use at the end of every task. In doing so, it'll allow you to release tension and lower your internal pressure, and as a result, you'll be far less reactive, less stressed and more composed. I actually got this idea from a practice they teach A&E doctors and nurses in the NHS (the British health service) to deal with crisis situations. In those moments, it's normal for adrenaline, panic and stress to kick in, which is why it's vital they calm down before making decisions or taking action. While different scenarios, the response to dealing with fires for CEOs can in many ways trigger the same response. That's why I tested a tweaked concept out on myself and then with clients, and it was so effective, it became a staple tool in the arsenal of my Evolved program ever since.

The reason being is whenever you're facing those challenges all that stress builds up inside you and it pushes you into a heightened state. During this time, your blood pressure increases and your cortisol levels go up. Which as a result, explain why at times you may get brain fog or struggle to keep focus. The reality is there's no way you can make the right decisions, execute at your best, or lead your team when you feel this way – yet this is the state of mind that most overwhelmed CEOs operate from for most of their days.

This technique breaks that cycle, as it forces you to stop, slow down and breathe. This action lowers your blood pressure and cortisol levels, all while calming you down and restoring you to a cleared-headed focus.

How to do the Stress De-compounding Technique

Stop what you're doing, if possible close your eyes, and from there, take a deep breath in to the count of four, then out to the count of four. In to the count of four, then out to the count of four.

Focus on your breathing and imagine that with every exhale, you're letting go and pushing out the built-up tension inside of you.

You want to continue doing this for anything from 60 to 120 seconds, however, I've found the sweet spot generally tends to be about 90 seconds. After a while of practicing this you'll notice what works for you, and that'll allow you to judge when you feel ready to stop.

Now the reason why this is so effective is because facing those stressors throughout the day causes the tension to build up inside you. Doing this at the end of every task will allow you to regularly release that tension. Think back to the gas tank example I gave you, as it's essentially like opening the tap and letting some gas out. Doing so will allow you to recalibrate and ground yourself throughout the day, and as a result, you'll feel far less reactive to setbacks and more in control of your emotions when things go wrong.

When you then combine this with resetting your intention, it'll be a complete game-changer for how you feel throughout the day.

As picture this, you've just had a really intense board meeting, where you come out full of adrenaline and on edge. Now, instead of taking that stress with you into that next client call or writing project, how much better would you feel if you stopped, let it all out, refocused your intention and only dived into what's next when you feel calm and relaxed? That's the entire point of this exercise, as it's forcing you to ground yourself throughout the day and in doing so, allowing you to feel far more in control.

Not only that, but do you know how some days you just feel exhausted? Your energy's depleted and you feel mentally tapped out, yet when you look at the clock it's not even 3 pm? This is something that happens to overwhelmed CEOs all the time. The problem with constantly rushing around, barely stopping to think, let alone breath, is that it causes all that tension to build up inside you. Which in turn, drains you mentally and emotionally. That's why by taking those few moments throughout the day to stop, breathe and reset your intention, you'll find that come the end of the day, you'll feel far more energized as well.

As a recap, here's what to do at the end of every big task:

1) Stop, close your eyes if possible and for 60 to 120 seconds take big, deep breaths, in to the count of four, and out to the count of four. Focus on your breathing and imagine that with every exhale you're releasing that built-up tension.

2) Once you feel calmer and grounded, then reset your intention. Take a couple of minutes to think about what's next and mentally take yourself through the task. Think about what you need to get done. What outcome do you want to create? What challenges may come up along the way? And how do you need to handle them as the best version of yourself?

This won't take more than a few minutes. And you'll find that this focused, intentional time will completely transform everything from your productivity, to how you deal with fires, your ability to stay calm under pressure and how you feel throughout the day.

Section 4

Taking control of your CEO role

Controlling the controllable

We've covered a lot so far on how to set yourself up in the best possible way to succeed. However, it's important to note that even with the best planning and preparation in the world, things can and will go wrong. It's merely part of the life of a CEO, as in everything you do there will always be challenges and setbacks, or elements that are simply out of your control.

Despite the uncertainty though, the evolved CEOs who are still able to feel in control of their role recognize that these challenges come with the territory. Which is why they realize that in order to handle them, they need to double down on focusing on their mindset and emotional control. After all, this is what's going to help keep them composed, and by arming themselves with the right psychology, tools and support, they can quickly bounce back, even when things do go wrong.

That's why one of the first shifts I instil in all of my clients is the realization that while you're never going to be in complete control of what's going on around you, the one thing you can always control is how you choose to respond to unpredictable situations. For me, it's an incredibly fulfilling part of the journey, as it's always amazing seeing them gain a newfound confidence, where they know that when faced with challenges or hard times, they can tackle them and get through. This happened recently for a client in our fourth session, where upon reflecting on his progress he said to me: "I realized that no matter what the situation, my response doesn't have to be reactive or emotional and it doesn't have to mess up my day." However, because overwhelmed CEOs haven't yet done the mindset and emotional control work needed to become an evolved CEO, this is where they become unravelled. As when issues start to arise, or their planning goes off course, they start to spiral into a whirlwind of emotional decisions, overthinking or procrastination, which at times can even have an almost paralysing effect. The reason being is they become so consumed by focusing on what went wrong, that all the negative energy and built-up tension stops them in their tracks. So rather than focusing on what they need to do about it, instead, they keep focusing on what happened or is out of their control. This in turn can cause the self-doubt to sink in, where they feel in over their head, start to second guess themselves, or wonder if they'd be better off just giving up.

Your identity and how you view yourself

A huge part of this mentality and how we're affected by these challenges comes down to our identity and how we view ourselves. As when you're truly passionate about what you do and it's a huge part of your life, it's normal for your business to become intertwined and a part of who you are. This however can be a huge problem, especially if you allow your business to define you, as in doing so you can get caught in the trap of viewing the businesses success as a direct reflection of who you are as a person. Because have you ever felt like when things are going badly, it's you who's a failure or not good enough? Or worse still, because you set such high standards and expectations of yourself, that even when things are going well, you still feel like you could be doing better? This is directly tied to your identity and the way in which it's causing you to view yourself. One of the big realizations I've made, is that you are not your business, even though at times it can be hard to tell them apart.

In order to break this cycle, we have to focus on upgrading our identity. By shifting your focus from the business and instead placing it within, you can become clear on not just who you are, but also who you need to become to create the life and success you want. For evolved CEOs, this is the first step towards taking control of the life they want, as they recognize that to break through to the next level, they firstly need to grow and evolve within themselves.

The truth about running a business

Regardless of that internal growth though, the life of a CEO certainly isn't for the faint of heart. Especially when you can do everything right, give your business your all and sacrifice everything to make your dreams a reality, yet still come up short.

I remember one time in particular in my own business where for weeks we'd been working on a huge campaign and getting ready for launch. I put everything I had into it and I truly believed this was going to be the moment where all my hard work paid off and my business would break through to the next level. Yet come launch day, it completely failed. I remember having this sinking feeling within myself and I'll never forget walking into my kitchen, where all of a sudden, I just couldn't hold it in anymore, and I just broke down in the corner. I just didn't know what to do. I'd given it my all, yet still, it hadn't worked. Looking back in that moment, I had a choice. I could have easily just thrown in the towel and quit, going back to a job and returning to a lower stress, comfortable life. But after a few minutes, I got up, shook myself off and carried on, as for me it didn't feel like a choice at all, as I knew I had to find another way.

Now, this wasn't the first time, and it won't be the last either, as the unfortunate reality is that in the game of being an entrepreneur, there are no guarantees. That's why I believe you need to be a special kind of crazy to be a CEO, as you're basically signing up for a life where the daily setbacks can feel like a punch in the gut, where every day you need to pick yourself up and come back for more. This is also why CEOs and business owners are my favourite type of people, as despite all the odds stacked against them, that burning desire to change and impact the world still pushes them to persevere and go after what they want.

Like I said before though, as a CEO you're never going to be in complete control of what's going on around you, but the one thing you can always control is how you choose to respond to it. That's why one of the most powerful traits of an evolved CEO is being able to see a challenge, understand what's going on and detach the feelings that come with it. Where instead of being pulled into fires or making decisions from a state of reaction, they can stop, understand what's going on and control how they respond to it. While it's true some people are born with more conviction than others, I've found that this state of mind can be learned and developed.

I made this discovery the hard way during a period of my business where all the days of responding to challenges in front of me and just trying to make it through the day had taken its toll. I remember one night in particular just lying in bed with a feeling of dread over facing another day of fires, solving people's problems and never-ending demands. It was exhausting, and I realized that if something didn't change, then I didn't know if I could or if I wanted to do this any longer.

That moment was a turning point for me, as I had seen countless examples of successful CEOs who were able to handle the pressures that came with their success, so I knew there had to be a way. This set me off down a path of learning everything I could about psychology, mindset and high-performance, determined to figure out what it takes to perform at the highest level.

What I discovered was that those CEOs who had not only reached the top of the mountain, but were able to sustain it as well, had mastered three key areas: their mindset, emotional control and performance. As by evolving within themselves, this was how they unlocked the ability to show up as a confident and powerful leader who can make timely decisions, handle the stress of running a business and inspire those around them. This was how they became that next level, evolved CEO.

Now, the purpose of this book has been all about performance, in giving you the tools and strategies you need to take back control of your time and free yourself up from your business. And everything in here works, as long as you implement it and follow through.

Have you ever thought about why you can give 100 people the exact same strategy, yet they all get vastly different results?

Well, if the strategy is the same, then what's the difference?

The biggest differences are the mindset and emotional control of the person trying to execute the strategy. After all, the perfect strategy or plan is meaningless if you're spending your days in a reactive state, feeling stressed and overwhelmed, if you're overthinking decisions, doubting yourself or not having the confidence to execute on what you need to get done.

And this is where so many overwhelmed CEOs get caught in the trap of focusing on the wrong areas of growth. Convincing themselves the reason why things aren't working is because they have the wrong strategy or need more tactics. I'll be the first to admit how much I fell into this trap in the past, as I spent so much time bouncing around between books, courses and training programs, hoping I'd find the magical secret that would turn it all around. It was only when I stopped and did the inner deep work that I realized the biggest barrier in the way was myself. It was that sabotaging voice in my head, and my inability to deal with the challenges that came with my success. This was the real reason why my role as a CEO felt out of my control.

Obviously having the right strategy is important, but what I found was that the evolved CEOs who recognize the need to grow within themselves by building an internal foundation around the three core pillars of mindset, emotional control and performance were the ones who are able to take those strategies and execute them at the highest level. It's what gives them their edge and enables them to consistently show up at their best, all while keeping it together in the face of adversity.

The reason being, is each pillar directly impacts the others:

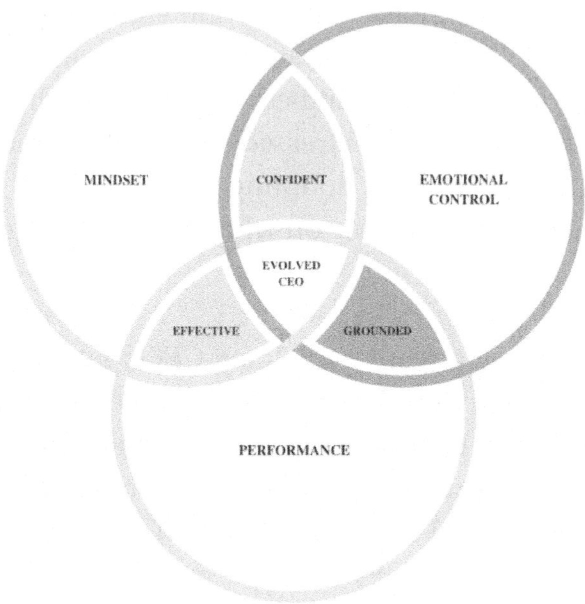

What I've found is that most overwhelmed CEOs tend to just focus on one or possibly two of these pillars. Which is a huge issue, because:

You can have the right mindset and be super productive, but if you can't control the stress or deal with the pressure, it's going to keep you trapped in a reactive state of fight or flight where you're controlled by your emotions.

Or you can be really organised and grounded, but if you don't believe in yourself, then you'll keep second-guessing what you're doing, avoiding making decisions and not taking the actions you know you need to take.

Or you can mentally and emotionally be in the right place, but if you don't know how to manage and defend your time, then you'll spend your days stretched thin and feeling like no matter what you do, you're always behind.

Now, if your role currently feels out of your control and you're not performing at the level that you want, I'd be willing to bet you're missing one or more of these pillars.

That's why in order to become an evolved CEO, we need to build a foundation of all 3. As when you get them in alignment, that's when you'll be able to tap into your full potential. This is how you evolve into that next level, more confident, grounded and effective decision-making leader, who can handle the pressures of running and growing a business.

It's important to note, that ensuring these foundations are built and strengthened becomes even more important as your business grows. After all, with every new level of success, comes a new level of problems, which is why the level of thinking, emotional control and performance that got you to where you are now, isn't going to be enough to sustain this level of success, let alone breakthrough to the next level.

Think of it like this:

Remember your old laptop and how when you first got it, it worked great? It was really fast, and could handle everything you needed it to…

Yet after a while, didn't it start to slow down? Its memory wasn't as good as it used to be? It struggled handling multiple tasks at any one time and if you put too much pressure on it then it would crash and stop working? What most people don't realize, is that our brains work in a similar way. Which is why for so many overwhelmed CEOs, the deeper problem is that their brains' internal operating system simply can't keep up with the demands that come with the new levels of their success.

The biggest bottleneck in most businesses

One of my clients is a perfect example of this in action. He first reached out to me when his business was going through a period of explosive growth. Yet despite all the exciting things going on around him, he found himself in a situation where all of a sudden, he also had to lead and manage a team, keep stakeholders happy and overlook the day-to-day operations. It was a huge amount to stack on top, and between all the fires, problems and demands, he was feeling stretched thin, in over his head and on a rollercoaster ride of emotions.

Like so many other overwhelmed CEOs, he was spending his days in a constant state of response, where everything he did was in reaction to what was going on around him. And this was a huge issue, as because he was stuck in his own head, decisions weren't being made, projects were becoming stalled and opportunities were being lost, all because he wasn't being as effective as he needed to be as a CEO.

You see, the problem was that while his business had grown, internally he'd stayed the same. Which was why the level of thinking, action and brainpower that got him to where he was, simply wasn't able to keep up with the new demands added to his CEO role.

This is a perfect example of why the bottleneck for most businesses is not the wrong strategy, team or market conditions and instead, it's the mindset and emotional control of the CEO.

Let me say that again. **The bottleneck for most businesses is the mindset and emotional control of the CEO.**

Can you see why if you're currently feeling or performing this way it's not your fault? It's just that the level of thinking, emotional control and performance that got you to where you are now, is struggling to keep up with the demands that come with your new levels of success.

Which raises the question: what's the solution?

As you've seen above, **your business's growth can't outgrow your inner growth**. Which is why in order to break through to the next level of impact, income and success, like that old laptop computer, you need to upgrade, to **evolve**.

For that client I just mentioned, that meant taking the time to focus on evolving his mindset, emotional control and performance to the next level. In doing so, he was able to get the clear-headed focus to make better decisions, the confidence to execute without overthinking and the emotional control needed to handle the stress and pressure that came with his success. As a result, his business has continued to grow, bringing in more investment, taking new products to market and furthering his mission of making the world a better place.

So how do we do it?

The purpose of this book was all about giving you the tools you need to hone your focus and prioritize your time, so that you can become a more effective CEO. Because of that, diving into the mindset and emotional control aspect is beyond the realm of what we're focusing on.

However, I did still want to show you the bigger picture of what's actually involved in getting you to show up and perform at your best, as like I said, this is something I wish someone had told me about back when I was struggling on my own. Instead, I had to spend years going through my own journey, spending thousands of hours researching, tens of thousands of dollars on courses and certifications, as well as thousands of hours trying to figure out how to achieve that inner growth.

Eventually, I figured out what it takes to go from feeling stressed, overwhelmed and not performing at your potential, to becoming that next level more confident, grounded and effective, decision making leader. And in doing so, I developed a proven 5-step process in order to create that transformation. Over the last few years, I've been using that process to help CEOs and business leaders from around the world take control of their role, so that they can perform at a higher level.

Now you're obviously here for a reason, part of you knows you're meant for so much more, which is why if it's ok with you I'd love to take a moment to talk to you about how I can help you beyond this book.

Because imagine this...

Imagine waking up in 90-days and from the moment you start your day instead of feeling overwhelmed by a never-ending to-do list, knowing exactly what to focus on and prioritize. With the right systems in place to manage your time, effectively delegate and ensure that instead of getting stuck in your own head, you can consistently take the actions you need to take.

Imagine having the clear-headed focus to make better decisions and the confidence to know that regardless of the challenge in front of you, that you can handle it and get through. Where even if things do go wrong, you can trust your own intuition, stay emotionally stable and despite the chaos going on around you, remain calm, have clarity and feel in control.

Imagine that rather than your days consumed by fires or reacting to problems, that you could get out of the trenches and finally step into the role of the CEO you need to become to take your business to the next level. Where you can reflect on your days knowing that the work you did grew the business, furthered your vision and created more revenue and impact.
Imagine feeling in control of your life and business. Where when you do take time off you can be present, feel connected to those around you and finally enjoy the freedom you worked so hard for.

And imagine that instead of feeling like you were in this on your own, you had someone in your corner and a prop that you could lean on so that you don't have to get into the ring alone.

Because here's the thing. You don't need to imagine this happening, as I want to help you turn this into a reality.

From everything we've covered in this book, do you think that if you spent the next few months, or even 12 months with me coaching you, do you think that would have a positive impact on your performance as a CEO, your life and the success that you could create?

If the answer is yes, then there are two options. If you want support working directly with me, then my Evolved program may be a great fit. Alternatively, if you'd rather do it on your own, then my Unshakeable course will take you step by step through everything you need to know.

Both will help you take control of your role so that you can break through to the next level. The big difference obviously, is the amount of direct support you receive. I'll give you an overview of both, and from there you can decide which path is right for you.

The Evolved program

The Evolved program is for first time CEOs who feel overwhelmed by the challenges that come with running and growing a business.

Using my battle-tested 5-step Evolved Method, I want to help you become the CEO your business needs now and in the future.

By the end, you'll change the way you think, how you process problems and navigate challenges.

You'll make better decisions, be able to trust your intuition and lead with confidence.

And a result, you'll feel more in control of your life and business.

As you become the CEO you need to be to create more growth, make more impact and have more freedom to enjoy the success you worked so hard for.

The Evolved Method has been implemented by CEOs in 14 different countries. Ranging from founders to CEOs growing tech companies, 7-figure agencies, global production companies and billion-dollar unicorns in Silicon Valley.

Due to the high level of support in this program, joining is by application only. To apply for a place drop me an email at **byron@byronmorrison.com** and we can set up a call to see if working together is the right fit

Alternatively, you can find out more at:

https://www.byronmorrison.com/evolved-program

What my clients have to say

On my website I have a section for client video case studies and testimonials sharing their thoughts from working together. You're welcome to go check them out in full at

www.byronmorrison.com, but here are some extracts from what my clients had to say about working with me, after going through this Evolved transformation:

Jordan (CEO): *"When I first started working with Byron, I really didn't feel like I was where I wanted to be. I felt like things were out of control, I didn't know how to get my life of working 80 hours and was struggling to spend enough time with my family. I was really trying to get that back, and what I found was that so much of what I didn't feel in control of, I had the ability to get in control of by changing the way I thought about things, by changing the way I approached situations, how present I was, having a true vision for my future, having action plan that really allowed me to recapture that control, to get organised, to come into meetings and be with my family, everything improved."*

Ron (CEO): *"After working with Byron and him offering the tools and rewiring my mindset, I have now come back as a more confident leader, I have learned how to defend my schedule, I've learned how to be less reactive, but to also to be able to just pause and look at situations and come up with a better plan, a better solution. I've set new standards…and I'm very confident that Byron is going to change your life for the better"*

Max (Tech CEO): *"Honestly, it's been one of the best decisions I've made. Certainly, compared to the financial investment the value that's come out of it has been astounding."*

Tyler (Business owner): *"I feel like I've left this universe and gone into a different one. It's been incredible…If you judge my level of happiness, clarity, sleep cycle, relationships, confidence, or every other area of my life, it's an easy win. My direction in life has completely changed"*

Rosemary (Business leader): *"I don't feel like I have control back, I feel like I have it for the first time. I used to be fighting all these fires and battles and it was exhausting. As everything felt out of my control and I was miserable. Now I feel calm and like that fire is merely a distraction that I know I can handle."*

Michael (CEO): *"I've gone from completely tired, exhausted, drained to back to my old self so to speak and with more purpose. I'm glad I did it, I certainly know that if I didn't, I'd probably still be in that state of unhappiness and stress. It was the best money I've ever spent on myself"*

Neil (Business owner): *"I now feel completely different, I feel clear-headed and able to focus on the stuff I work out that I should be focusing on, I don't jump around anywhere near as much...I'm in control"*

Josh (Business leader): *"People around me recognised that I'm* more effective than I've ever been"

Are you next? Find out more and set up a time to speak directly to Byron to see if it is the right fit at:
https://www.byronmorrison.com/evolved-program

The Unshakeable Course

If you want to take this a step further, but you're not ready for direct support, want a more cost-effective option or you want to do it on your own, then my Unshakeable Course is the next best thing to working directly with me. This 6-week course is going to help you master the mental game needed to be a highly effective CEO. I'll take you step by step through upgrading your identity, mastering your emotions, solidifying the right routines, getting you out of your own head and breaking through the beliefs that are holding you back.

I'll also be sharing tools and techniques with you that I've never shared outside of the work with my private clients. Giving you everything you need to take control of your life and business and as a result, making you a more grounded, confident and effective CEO.

As a thank you for purchasing this book, I've put together a special offer for you to access the "Unshakable" course at a reduced investment. You can find out more and get started at:

www.byronmorrison.com/unshakeableoffer

Summary

I know we've covered a lot in this book, from uncovering your zone of genius to defending your time, how to structure your days and ensuring you execute at the highest level. One thing I really want to take a moment to highlight though, is you. Most people talk about wanting to get better, they buy books, enrol in courses and talk about all the things they're going to do. Yet when it comes down to it, they rarely follow through. By finishing this book though you've proven that isn't you, and that's amazing, so I don't want you to overlook that. I have no doubt incredible things are in store for you and I'd love to know more about what you're working on and what's going on in your world. So feel free to get in touch to share your story with me and connect, or if you have any questions about this book or the high-performance space, I'm also happy to help.

You can connect with me or follow my content at:

LinkedIn:

https://www.linkedin.com/in/authorbyronmorrison/

Facebook:

https://www.facebook.com/byronmorrisonauthor/

Or alternatively, drop me an email at **byron@byronmorrison.com** and I'll personally respond.

Leave a review

Like I wrote at the start of this book, my mission is to evolve CEOs into who they need to become to change the world. Which is why I believe that by getting them to take control of their role, they will be able to create a greater impact and change the lives of others for the better.

As with any mission though, I can't do it on my own. So if you enjoyed this book, it would mean the world to me if you'd take a moment to leave a review on Amazon to help spread the word.

Join our community

I believe that being part of a community and surrounding ourselves with the right people plays a vital role in our success. That's why as part of furthering my mission I'm creating a community for impact driven CEOs to meet others, find inspiration, share stories and get support.

This is also going to be your go to place to exchange ideas with other CEOs, share challenges, get support and continue your growth.

It's free to join, so if you haven't already you can join the community at:

https://www.facebook.com/groups/impactdrivenceos

Final thoughts

That's it, we've reached the end and I just want to say a huge thank you. I hope you enjoyed reading this book as much as I enjoyed writing it.

If you want to dive more into the mindset aspect of being a highly effective CEO, then you can also get the next book in the series "CEO In Control" on Amazon.

Again, thanks for reading and whether we work together directly or cross paths in our community, I look forward to getting to know you better and finding more about your journey.

Byron Morrison

Get my new book

I'm excited to announce my next book – "Maybe You Should Give Up – 7 Ways To Get Out Of Your Own Way And Take Control Of Your Life".

Inside Maybe You Should Give Up you'll discover 7 ways to get out of your own way, so that you take control of your life. The book is all about putting an end to self-sabotage, so that you can break through everything that is stopping you from living the life you want.

Pre-order now at Barnes and Noble or Waterstones and email a screenshot of the receipt to **byron@byronmorrison.com** and I'll send you access to AMPLIFY as a thank you.

I also have various other bonuses including copies of my other books, free access to my other courses, consulting time and private workshops for your team if you order bulk copies.

Find out more at
www.byronmorrison.com/maybeyoushouldgiveup

Printed in Great Britain
by Amazon